THE CHEF'S
RECOVERY

BY TV'S THANKFULLY LOCAL CHEF

CHUCK HAYWORTH

D1158592

This book is intended to supplement, not replace, the advice of a trained health professional. If you know or suspect that you have a health problem, you should consult a health professional. The author and publisher specifically disclaim any liability, loss or risk, personal or otherwise, that is incurred as a consequence, directly or indirectly, of the use and application of any of the contents of this book.

Printed in the United States of America

First Edition, 2014

ISBN 978-0-9896359-4-3

For more information please visit www.TheChefsRecovery.com

· DEDICATION ·

Dedicated to all those great folks who have helped me in my recovery including, but not limited to: my loving family, all my friends in Miami, especially Cathy & Danny Reyes, Adam, and all those who shared their stories with me in the oncologist's office, many of whom have lost their battle to this dreaded disease of cancer. I will not rest until this disease is eradicated from the face of the Earth and the next generation shall not suffer from this ailment!

· CONTENTS ·

· PART ONE ·

THE STORY

· CHAPTER 1 ·

JUST BEFORE

I grew up in the small town of High Point, North
Carolina, a town whose foundation was and still remains
rooted in the furniture industry. Back in the 1980s,
you could smell the distinct scent of furniture finishes
wafting from downtown and even the smell of tobacco
toasting to our west from Winston-Salem. Growing up,
it was overwhelming to constantly hear my family name
mentioned around town, as the Hayworth factories
employed much of the population. Ironically, the presence
of so many buildings and structures bearing our name
gave me the motivation to make my mark elsewhere.

In my opinion, the 1990s were the last of the great
years of North Carolina's industrial revolution. Change
came quickly with NAFTA, and so did the end of furniture
manufacturing as we knew it in High Point. We would
remain the "Furniture Capital of the World," but the town

would lose some of the charm achieved by the greatest generation's hard work.

The early '90s were a great time for our family, too. My father chose to attend law school because of the unwelcome changes in the furniture manufacturing industry. My two brothers each chose unique career paths in their own ways. My fun-loving younger brother Mike was working toward a career in film. My older brother, Joe, was the intellectual one and was always studying and spending his time reading and researching Lincoln-Douglas Debates tactics. This remarkably led to a career in sales as opposed to politics. Where did that leave me? What about Chuck?

I was the ever-social romantic! In the eighth grade, I had a wrestling injury which ended my hopes of lettering in anything in high school. However, I discovered a great love for writing, drawing, theater, and journalism. I also discovered a love for all things photography! This meant that for nearly four years, if someone wanted to contact me, they knew I could be found in either the darkroom in my high school, or the bathroom darkroom which my father and I had created in our basement . My father insisted I begin working at the local small town photo shop because if I wasn't in a dark room, I was usually there purchasing equipment. I never went anywhere in my four years of high school without my camera equipment. It landed me a place with the school newspaper, with the yearbook, and a ticket to every hot party or event around town! I also made side money taking pictures of events around town. Chances are, if it was an event involving anyone from High

Point during this time period, I shot a picture of it. Some of my greatest moments were political campaigns and state basketball and football championships because I was among the real media, not just school reporters.

Everyone eventually reaches the point where high school comes to an end. Like most seniors, I had no idea what to do next. I had friends suggest culinary school but I laughed my head off at the idea. And so I did what was expected of me after high school, I enrolled in the local university.

That worked for only one semester. I had way too much fun there and then transferred to a local community college to start photography courses. Unfortunately, everywhere I went in the area my name followed me. I struggled in the university arena as well as the local community college environment to live up to my own expectations and those of the professors—many who knew my father or mother and even other family members, which would not provide any break for me. Oftentimes in social gatherings it made it quite difficult to determine who was a true friend and who was trying to use me for my community standing. My family has had a great influence in the local university as well as around town in various services such as the hospital. In short, the name was and is everywhere. The furniture company my family started was once the top employer in the city. I found myself struggling for my own identity as many young men in their late teens and early twenties often do, only multiplied by my family's influence in the community. I often joke that flunking out of community college and being told by my parents to "get a job" was the best thing that could have happened to me.

I turned my focus toward foodservice and have never looked back. I started as a server's assistant (a.k.a. busboy) since I had little experience. I had never had to think about job experience and a resume. This was the "swallow my pride" moment that I believe everyone must have in order to move forward. I could finally be judged by a resume and not by my name. My self-esteem was at a low and was something that with maturity I would regain. At this point it was time to learn what hard work and determination were in pursuit of my new dream, a dream to open my own business away from High Point. With my family's business history, the entrepreneurial spirit was something which was instilled in me and at which I could thrive. I had to learn hospitality management strategy from the best, so I enrolled in business courses at my local community college and humbly moved home for a few months. Of course, the stress of trying to live up to the family name led to an addiction of two things, cigarettes and coffee.

Nothing gives you perspective in your early twenties like moving home. No temptations exist such as those found in one's dorm room or college apartment. While other friends and acquaintances were living the traditional college life, I was still trying to discover what I truly wished to achieve in my career. Back when I was having fun being the life of the party, I never thought of a career. Now would be different. I would use the opportunity to save as much money as I could to get my own place and move out of the bar and restaurant I was practically living in—a move toward the career path in resorts and hotels which I strongly desired.

Life in my parents' home was short-lived. I moved out shortly after taking a job as a front desk clerk at a major hotel chain. I had given a resume to a career fair representative earlier in the school year, a move which had finally paid off. This opened doors for me to travel while picking up shifts around the Southeast. Being privy to decisions made by corporate America and belonging to a hotel team was great. Part of what made the hospitality industry thrive at that time was the empowerment of employees, a trait I would incorporate into my own business model many years in the future. I learned a lot about what it took to be successful in corporate life while you are low in the chain of command. I loved working all-night shifts on the weekends because they paid more, and I could use the time to collect my thoughts of what to do with life next. It was during this time that I picked up shifts in foodservice and housekeeping to add to my resume, of which I was becoming increasingly proud. I learned to love saving my money and only used it to pay for tuition and books and the occasional meal or drink. I was determined to make something of myself. However, I saw opportunity after opportunity passing me by since I didn't have a college education. By the time I realized how important it was, many of my peers were graduating college and starting careers or graduate school. I was 22 years old and a recent retiree of a 2-pack-a-day habit when my life would change before I could blink.

One very late night, an admissions representative checked in. We talked for quite a while. He told me I should apply to hospitality schools and culinary schools across the country and see if I get in. I did just that and wrote a humbling essay. I was accepted to the Miami campus of Johnson and Wales University among several other universities across the country. From the ashes of humility—and a lot of swallowed pride—came the largest lifestyle change I ever had to make.

· CHAPTER 2 ·

STOMACH CANCER

As I boarded the flight to Fort Lauderdale, I was determined to experience life as far from the familiar as possible. If this small town boy was going to be successful, I would have to learn about ingredients with which I was unfamiliar, expose myself to various cultures, and, most of all, learn and respect the classic European styles and techniques taught in this culinary program.

When I arrived in Miami, I assumed it was like any other place in the South. I was absolutely wrong. The people were completely different. There were so many different languages and dialects spoken that I lost track. Still, I settled into housing and made the best of living with people that were an average of four to five years younger than I was. I think I was the only student to read the local paper as well as two national publications before class every day. I found myself reading about travel and tourism as well as local foods and markets around Miami and the entire state of Florida. Unlike most of my fellow dormmates, I genuinely cared about what was going on in the world and how it might affect my chosen career path. Looking back, these young people were in the same soul-searching stages of their lives from which I had just made a transition.

I was able to really experience the sights and smells of Miami my first year in culinary school because I relied on public transportation. Utilizing public transportation in a large metropolitan city like Miami would help me become engulfed in the culture and sights. This seemed like a gateway to a new life full of new experiences. One night I was all alone and decided to board the bus that headed through the district I called "the tourist district" in Miami. The simple glow of the neon lights of the Raleigh Hotel proved to be mind-boggling. I began to feel doubt about leaving North Carolina and remember feeling tears fall down my face. Drying my tears, I realized these were thoughts that would understandably take place in the mind of a small town boy who had just moved to the big city. It was the first year of a new millennium in 2001. Finally, I was going to make something of my new university and new home.

On the right day, you could smell the ocean in the distance along with Cuban espresso in the air; it had a very Parisian effect on my senses. This city would be my Paris, and culinary school would prove to be my canvas; a way of starting fresh as an artist starts every brush stroke like they are stroking the first brush full of paint. It is important to note that my accent stuck out like a sore thumb. I was a long way from home (by choice), like a drifter longing for a new place to call home. Every step I took and every block I traveled felt as if it were new to me. Even the smallest high-rises looked huge to me! Somehow, looking back, I still consider Northern Miami-Dade and South Broward home. At least, it was the first place I would call home. The healing powers of South Florida would provide hope that life beyond North Carolina did exist and they would prove to be exactly what I needed to mend my confidence and find a new identity. South Florida would ultimately prove to aid in the healing process of something far more serious than the obvious self-esteem issues and career path quest.

The first few weeks of culinary school flew by! The whole world around me changed just the second week of culinary school. The attacks on the World Trade Center in New York, The Pentagon, and Pennsylvania were a devastating blow to our nation which I love so dearly. However, for me, they provided the first feelings of utter helplessness I had ever known: strong, genuine desires to help in my new community followed by the guilt of not being by my family's side during this time of national mourning and unity. For the first time ever I was alone with no one. Classes were canceled and school phone lines were tied up with so many students, foreign and domestic, calling home to check in with families and friends who were possibly affected by the tragedy. It was not until several days later that you could smell the soot and ash in the air in the city of Miami wafting its way down the Eastern coastline. It was a time in our history

I will never forget. Time moved by so quickly in Miami. There were flags on fire trucks and people donating plasma and food; people genuinely wanting to help their fellow man. I have never seen a large metropolitan area so alive and unified as the citizens of Miami were during that week. These killers were traced to a flight school in South Florida. All of the sudden, my new community felt more like the small town I had just left. This would prove to be short-lived.

Classes resumed and everything was moving quickly with the introduction to new ingredients, methods of cooking, sauces, stocks and cuts of meats. There was a bombardment of information coming from "seasoned chefs" with letters after their names—letters that I later learned were certifications such as CMC, CEC, CPC, etc. I was a small town boy in a big city school trying to fit in. Just a few weeks into culinary school, I started to second-guess myself, wondering, *am I in the right place? Maybe I should have gone to culinary school at home.* The "seasoned chefs" informing me of my ignorance and lack of knowledge of the simple basics would prove to not weaken, but nourish and strengthen my inner desire to someday hold the coveted title of Chef. Suddenly, I heard my inner voice sounding like David Bowie singing "turn and face the stranger," and it finally hit me—I was studying in a tropical paradise! It was the mental mise en place boost which I so desperately needed.

It was my mother who told me that I could not hold a job and go to school because that proved over time to be a major factor in my failing out of college in the first place. Like the "seasoned chefs" I had encountered in the beginning of culinary school, my mother's tough love would solve an inner riddle and would prove to be a great motivator. As a result, I would go to class during the week, practice on the weekends with the part-time students, and volunteer for every culinary event that I could attend around town. Although these were not paid opportunities, they were more valuable than any paid position I ever had as I won the hearts and minds of many of the "seasoned chefs" who organized these events around town. I would have one-on-one opportunities outside of school to share with them my passion for cooking and serving food. This not only opened the door for me with influential people in Miami and South Florida, but also proved to be a valuable way to go from ignorant to good graces of influential "seasoned chefs" which affected grades ultimately. It gave me the extra practice I needed, introduced me to some amazing friends and gave me a free meal!

About six weeks into school, I began to feel sick to my stomach. I remember having a great time with my friends without giving it much thought until Thanksgiving break. It was then that I realized something was really wrong. The occasionally annoying, sharp, needle-like piercing pain had turned into constant throbbing. It was definitely more than just something I ate or my serious addiction to café con leches from the nearby bodega.

Fueled by my mother's insistence, I went to visit my physician over Thanksgiving break. My hometown doctor was more of a friend than a physician. He was only a few years older than I was. He and I chatted about my love for all things sports and food. I would later say that everyone loves to eat; it's so easy to talk about food.

His diagnosis was that I had been exposed to the flu at school and that all would be better in a few weeks with a lot of rest and relaxation. I remember fearing that maybe during the course of our conversations I had missed telling him something. It is important to note that doctors are rarely presented with the full picture. We, as the patients, hold the entire story and it is up to us to share this with them! If only I had spoken up and insisted that I had the flu dozens of times and this was no flu. But still I remained silent and trusted my doctor's opinion. A huge lesson would be learned about communication with physicians which can only be attributed to experience and maturity.

The holiday was a blur. I cannot recall any details from that year except the tremendous pain I was feeling and the weakness that was setting into my ever-tiring body. When I boarded the plane back to South Florida, I remember thinking that I had not rested enough and may need a second opinion from a doctor I didn't know. The weeks that followed were touch-and-go. I could feel my body becoming frailer. I could barely keep my food down and was having severe cramps. My bowel movements were tar colored and hard as a rock. It was as if someone was taking a sharp knife and piercing my stomach with it. These symptoms were only temporarily soothed by over-the-counter pain medication given to me by my friends in the dorms.

My lowest point was the week I could barely move. Friends in school began to worry about how weak and frail

I was becoming. Are you ever hungry? Do you ever eat anything? At this point, it hurt to eat and drink. I was in Miami surrounded by great food and all I could long for was the comfort of my small city bed and North Carolina's sunshine and fresh air. The buzz of the seemingly carpe diem, artistic, Parisian effect had worn off. I even found myself longing for home so much that I would take the bus passing by the Raleigh hotel in Miami, hoping it would jog a faint memory of home sweet home. At the same time, I was adamant about staying and finishing the trimester—I didn't want to give up and just go home. Sticking to my guns, counting down the days until winter break, I found myself visiting the nurse's office more and more. The same explanation was given. I am going to give you some pain medicine and you should follow up with your home physician when we break for the holiday. The days became more excruciatingly painful and long. I felt like I was truly dying on the inside. The pain increased and I was becoming feverish.

When winter break finally arrived, I recall failing several midterms just to get out of town, to the airport and home. The dream of becoming a chef was slipping away. Strong feelings of hopelessness and guilt of possible failure set in and there was only one person to point to. The guy looking back in the mirror had turned a pale shade of white. The longest bus ride of my life was the ride to Fort Lauderdale airport that day! I felt so weak and tired. It was not too late to stop at the hospital on the bus trip up Biscayne Boulevard. A strong desire to exit the bus at the hospital emergency room is all I recall feeling. Instead of exiting the bus, I regrettably stared at the hospital's holiday decorations and lights. Instead, I boarded the Broward B Bus to the airport, connected at Aventura Mall, and continued on my long and tiresome trip. At each bus transfer, the drivers helped me hoist my long green canvas duffle bag onto the bus. I truly believe they all knew something was wrong.

Ordinarily this trip took twenty-five to thirty minutes; today it took almost an hour. Ahhh the bumper-to-bumper sounds and sights coupled with an orchestra of car horns and drivers creating their own traffic lanes— that is South Florida during the holiday season. The last thing I remember before passing out were the holiday decorations around the city of Fort Lauderdale. I awoke to the sound of the loud brakes of the bus. We were nowhere near the airport! Had I gotten on the wrong bus? With all the strength I could muster came a simple question, "Sir, are we stopping at the airport?"

"Yes sir, we have circled this route three times past the airport!" he responded. I looked down at the time on my prepaid cell phone. I had passed out for over an hour and a half!

"How long 'til we arrive at the airport again?" I asked the driver.

"Hard to tell; it's the holiday season in South Florida, buddy! The roads are packed and it depends on traffic." If ever there was a state of panic inside of me, I felt it at this moment.

Sulking back into my uncomfortable, half-plastic, half-thick-polyester-shag-coated chair, I began to feel my mother's disappointment that perhaps I had really messed up and missed my plane. *Maybe I'll spend my holiday in South Florida after all. No way can I afford another ticket.* I had less than twenty dollars in my pocket. My mother booked all my flights home while I was away at school. It was particularly important that I not disappoint her because I had explained to her several weeks earlier that I was still sick and considering going to an emergency room in Miami. She quickly responded by booking my plane reservation home with her frequent flyer miles and told me to wrap up midterm exams and come home immediately. How would I explain that I had missed my plane? How would I get back to North Carolina? All I wanted was to go and see the doctor and get this resolved once and for all.

As fate would have it, my flight to Atlanta was delayed. This was a good thing but it presented yet another challenge—getting a new flight to Greensboro from Atlanta. I was placed on standby in Atlanta and checked my bags through. The lines at the security gate were outrageously long! This was the first holiday season post-9/11, so this meant bag searches, liquid restrictions, and pat-downs for nearly everyone, including me. Staring at my North Carolina driver's license, I saw a different me. It was not the pale, sick, weak me, but rather an overly-confident kid who was ready to take on the world! If I could only feel like that again! Making the standby seat bound to Greensboro was a blessing. Now I began to worry about explaining to my parents how I failed nearly all my midterms just to reach the airport and get home. Would my family lecture me about how I should have chosen a culinary school a little closer to home? Would they insist on my withdrawal from Miami and staying home? Freezing, tired and feeling all alone, draped in my heaviest coat and an airline blanket, I arrived in Greensboro.

Nothing can describe the joy I felt when the plane touched down. I was home. It felt like hell was where I was headed, but I was home! It felt great to be back surrounded by the love of friends and family, especially my girlfriend at the time. "So how's Miami? I bet it's beautiful during the holidays! Is it true they decorate the palm trees instead of Christmas trees?" A bombardment of questions, but Mom remained quiet. "You look pale as a ghost." I responded that I felt like a ghost. "If you are not well by the day after Christmas, I will force you out of bed to the urgent care facility." "Mom, all I want is to sleep in my own bed and spend a little time with my girlfriend and our dog Moses." (We had adopted Moses from the pound the spring before I left for Miami.) I knew seeing them would make me feel better. I just needed a little bit of normal. Maybe I could convince her to move with me to Miami! Maybe we could start a life together down there. This scenario played over and over in my head. After all, she was the one who convinced me to move to a school in Miami. The culture, the people, the parties, and the beaches. I would long for it in the weeks and months to follow. But for now, I was home.

My mother has always loved having the entire family together during the holidays and around the dining room table. She loves to decorate the house, especially her table, for every holiday. Winter of 2001 would break this tradition. Despite the fact that I had made the hectic journey home and was sitting at her table, we both knew something was terribly wrong. My body was so weak and I was as white as paper. My girlfriend felt helpless and my inevitable hospitalization would prove to be too much for her in the weeks and months to come. My frustration in the early months of recovery coupled with her helpless feelings of not being able to say or do anything would lead to our separation. She chose to become a surgical nurse so that she would never feel that helpless again.

I owe my road to recovery to many people. However, I credit a young physician's assistant, who in all likelihood drew the short straw and had to work the early shift the day after Christmas, for saving my life. The first step in a long chain of events began this day after Christmas, 2001. (My mother would later retell this story on my cooking show for our viewing audience. She doesn't tell this story much, if ever.) The PA examined me and said we should report to the hospital immediately for an emergency transfusion. This told me that this was much more serious than we thought! I had a bleeding ulcer in my stomach and my hemoglobin was at four. The average adult male at my age and weight had a level of fourteen. As if I were not scared enough, I was rushed to a hospital room and immediately given 4 transfusions which lasted days. I had always donated since I was seventeen years old but never thought I would be a recipient.

What felt like a million x-rays and cat scans were taken before anything was explained to me or my family. True loneliness is when you are attached to an IV with a transfusion of blood running through you with another IV running dyes through your body. This caused sheer panic inside of me. Heat followed by chills, followed by an awful metallic taste in my mouth! "Please talk to me," was all I could mutter to the technicians.

"Your doctor has ordered these scans, Mr. Hayworth. Try to relax and breathe. Relax and breathe," they responded.

"Are you kidding me? I am in pain…it stings…what is this heating…cooling? What is going on? Someone talk with me! Tell me what the hell is going on!"

"Try to relax Mr. Hayworth!"

"I am sick and tired of this! Someone talk to me! Be human for Christ's Sake! What is going on?" I pleaded with them.

"Your doctors have ordered scans. We are trying to get scans of your body to see what is causing the bleeding in your stomach, sir," a senior technician responded. Suddenly and without warning, the confidence that all of this was a huge mistake had ended.

"Why couldn't someone tell me that an hour ago, when I was brought down here?" Silence in the room. They were behind some glass speaking through a microphone and I was being exposed to God knows what.

All I can remember is being told to relax. That is so hard to do when you have no idea what is wrong with your body. I think they may have tried to give me a sedative as well. Chalky, orange-flavored x-ray liquid became a regular part of my diet and it was not a good thing! I was ordered to chug nearly a gallon so they could scan my stomach over and over, and still no explanation of what was wrong. There were multiple doctor consultations and hallway chatter. "Hallway chatter" is where the doctors consult each other right outside of your room about cases, including your own, and you can clearly hear them. X-rays and scans were being viewed right out of the corner view that I had. Finally, some information! There was concern for an outlined area on the x-ray and CT scan projecting a large shadow.

After being greeted by my primary care physician, the one doctor that I knew, I was introduced to a gastrointestinal doctor who is still my doctor to this day. The consensus was that I would need both an endoscopy as well as a colonoscopy to see how serious it was. As I recall, I was still in full denial at this point. *This is not happening! It's a bad dream! Maybe it could still be an error in the x-ray and scans. Maybe I moved when they said to remain still. I don't think they need all of this. After all I have had my transfusion and I'm feeling great!* I remember them saying as soon as a room became available that they would wheel me down to the operating room for both procedures. These procedures are part of men's and women's preventative care and are usually recommended for those in their forties and fifties, but I was half that. Coincidentally, this very procedure would be broadcasted on NBC in 2002 when journalist Katie Couric had one performed for the whole world to witness due to the loss of her husband from colon cancer. Basically, the doctor sedates you and proceeds to scope your body in two separate ways. I heard "wow" from a doctor but with that, they increased my anesthesia and out I went. I had no idea how integral a roll this procedure would play in the course of my recovery.

When I woke up, the doctor explained that the procedure had gone well and that he had an answer for the now team of doctors that were overseeing this procedure. A few hours later, I was released from the hospital. It was a great feeling breathing the air again, but little did I know what was ahead of me would require all of my might and all of my strength.

I remember the call from the doctor like it happened yesterday. Two sets of doctors called my mother's home; one was my gastroenterologist and the other a surgeon. Both of them informed her that surgery would be needed. This would be the first conversation between my mother and the doctors where the word "tumor" was used and being the remarkable, strong, and faithful woman she was and is, she would be the messenger. As difficult as it was for her to break this news to me, the phone calls to come in the near future would prove even more burdensome.

 I would be returning to the hospital again. This time it would be for the removal of a tumor the size of a large lemon. When she finally told me, a million thoughts ran through my head. *I should never have smoked. I should have listened to those telling me I should lose weight and eat healthier. I should have worked harder at everything I had ever attempted in life! I should have.....* There was no turning back now.

It was late December. The joy of the upcoming New Year's holiday had turned as somber as the dreary, cloudy, drizzly weather outside. I tried showing no fear even though I was tearing up inside, crying about the obvious harsh reality. Three days before the surgery, I was asked by my family where I would like to eat out. I chose a great ribs place. If this is going to be my last meal, at least I would go out licking my fingers! I kept assuring everyone that I was okay and nothing would go wrong. I kept denying that a tumor was growing in my body and possibly spreading through my whole digestive system. The rest of the conversation was mostly about going home to Miami and buying a place close to the beach when I returned. I figured denial was the best and most positive way to deal with the news that I may be a cancer patient soon and if I survived the surgery I would need to change my lifestyle! Everyone seemed gloomy except me which was highly unusual around our table. We finished the meal and the next two days were a blur. I would be on a liquid diet for my last two days. It was during these final 48 hours that I would feel totally alone. Realizing that I had said a few things that I did not mean took a lot for me to admit. Sometimes when you face possible death like this, you have feelings and say things to push loved ones away. Those who truly love you and know your love will stay by your side through thick and thin. This daunting reality of the future was too much for my girlfriend, and the day of the surgery was the day I began to lose her. She had never seen my mean and depressed side, which came out when I realized this was in fact cancer.

Just as it had been before, my entourage of family and friends accompanied me to the surgical check-in.

I was taken back immediately. They bombarded me with questions: "When did you last eat? Drink? Current medications? Are you allergic to latex?" The questions went on for a while. In that cold, dark place, I remember feeling alone once more. This was it; all of my unhealthy decisions had caught up with me. Yet, in an instant, I felt an overwhelming, unexplained confidence that I could fight this and win! My faith in something higher would be my guiding light.

These feelings were interrupted by a sharp stab of another IV connection by the nurse, and the flow of what I like to call "the knock-out juice." The nurse said, "Mr. Hayworth, count backwards from 10..." and all I remember was reaching the number seven. I was past the point of no return. I could not take the beach route now. But, I could dream about it and that I did.

Words can hardly explain what going under the knife is like at twenty-two years old. Obviously, I have to go by what the doctors say happened next. It was supposed to be the removal of a stomach tumor, but it wound up being an experience I describe many years later as "putting a square peg into a round hole." The tumor had spread; they had to remove a third of my stomach, part of my small intestines, and my entire duodenum. It was what my physicians had described as "the worst case scenario." The opinion was that it appeared to be benign. Much to the surprise of the physicians involved, the pathology report came back a few days later stating that it was, in fact, malignant.

Waking up in the recovery room finally confirmed this was not a bad dream but rather reality. The first indication was the sharp obstruction of the breathing tube in my throat. It was as though someone was choking me from the inside with a sharp pinch of pain surrounding my entire neck region. I don't recall them inserting it, but this discomfort would prove to be the least of my worries. "Mr. Hayworth, when you are fully conscious, we will remove your breathing tube...count to three with me and cough the entire time—one, two, three." Gagging and coughing grasping for a sign of clean air, longing for the beaches of South Florida, I released a cough which produced the first pain as sharp as 1,000 knives penetrating my stomach! *What are those? Staples? When can I go home? What is this?*

"Try not to panic, sir. Reach up and grab the IV. This is your 'happy button'—it is your pain medication. If you would like a little more relief, just press it." It was a small button which I called "my little friend."

After what felt like forever, the nurse explained that she was going to take me from recovery to my hospital room. All I remember is the chill in the air and the transport elevator taking me to a room where my mother and father were waiting, along with a few concerned, close friends. I was still heavily medicated and a bit loopy. "Look at these staples. I look like a Halloween monster," was my response to the first sight of the scar, which would serve as a daily reminder to me of this event, as it poured a yellowish, staining, colored fluid. "Wow that surgery took a long time...did they get it all? Let's hope so Chuck!" It was the voice of my older brother, Joe. I was then greeted by the voice of my ever nervous father who voiced his opinion. "No one, not even the doctors, knew if it was all gone or if it would come back." Lacking the confidence of predicting the future, I responded with, "it's just another obstacle I have to overcome. This will not keep me from becoming a chef."

After a while of visiting with family and close friends, the surgeon arrived to explain what he had removed and that it would be sent off to pathology. The next step was to cut down on pain medications and get me walking around the floor to keep bed rash and possible clots from occurring. Liquid was oozing from me like I was a recently tapped oil well. I would ask about it and was told it was the aftereffect of such a large surgery. The realization of the pain and road ahead still haunts me to this day. *How will life get back to normal? Will I ever eat solid food and taste normal foods again? Is this all just a nightmare? Will I ever see the ocean again? Will my hell become these hospital walls, never to return to normal life again? What is going to happen?*

I attribute much of being able to get up and feel pain again to the moment where my surgeon was insulting me, trying with all his might to get me out of that hospital bed and walking. It was easy to get under my skin in those days. I opted to wait until my great friend, who was like an older brother to me, came to visit. David explained how he would "kick my ass" if I didn't get up and walk around with him. So, of course, I did exactly what he said! We had a lot to talk about. He wanted to know about Miami and school—a great distraction for both of us. As it turns out, we both needed one another that dreary winter day close to

New Year's Eve of 2001. My mother would later comment how "amazing it is to see how we were all in the cancer boat together and we love and care for each other in this tight knit community." It's true. Since that day, I truly feel a bond with all the people, families, and patients I meet in this cancer "boat" and community. David had spent a great deal of his free time at the hospital, comforting his mother and spending time with his father. His father was also fighting the cancer battle but it didn't look good for him. I think we both needed each other that week. I feared the worst for his father, but knew that I could not give up for his sake. We still, from time to time, discuss that day. He assures me that he did nothing, but I beg to differ. Sometimes when you feel like it is too much, the great deity sends a strong spirit into your life when you least expect it. David was just that for me! The darkness had cleared the room. I was determined; I was going to walk out of that hospital and battle this with all my might.

New Year's Eve of 2001 would be a great memory! My brothers were with me, along with most of my mother's closest friends. Along came David's mother dressed to the nines! She had been visiting her husband's room not far away and thought she could brighten up my New Year's Eve by bringing magazines and balloons along with nearly her whole family. With all the commotion and still a bit loopy, I promised that I would cook food for her (something that she jokingly informs me that I still owe her.) I was on a full liquid diet and specifically clear liquids! After all of the excitement and before the family left, I remember thinking I needed a sparkling beverage! It was New Year's Eve after all. Confident that my mother would not sleep well until I was resting, I slowly nudged her before leaving that night. "Mom could you check with the nurses and see if I might have a little Ginger Ale tonight for New Year's?" "Sure honey," she said. To my delight, the nurse brought me my requested "bubbly" and we rang in 2002 in a hospital room overlooking downtown High Point. I swore I would never do that again. As I helplessly watched city after city from around the country and world usher in a new year, I could not help but wonder what my friends were doing in Miami for New Year's Eve. I found myself closing my eyes and dreaming of the celebrations on the beach as well as in downtown and the Florida Keys. What a party that must have been. It would be a pleasure I would have to experience many years later. Instead I would settle for a two-day-old copy of *The Miami Herald* with which my father greeted me a few days later. He had discovered a news stand that carried major cities' newspapers just a day or two after print. It would be his unique way of dealing with the diagnosis. As a father now, I cannot imagine the pain he was feeling when he was informed of my diagnosis. I began to wonder where I would I be next year. I wondered if I would live to see next year.

It was time to set new goals. I would get well enough to first return to and then finish what I had started in Miami—the slow and tedious study of the culinary arts that would ultimately, someday, lead to the title of Chef. No matter what, I would eat my favorite foods again. I would become a chef, and make a difference! Step one was leaving that hospital room and walking on my own. After watching replays of fireworks from all over the world and country, I had had enough! Leaning my bed up as far as I could, pain flowing through my whole body from the stress unassisted, I sat up and draped my left foot over the bed, sharp pains penetrating my lower digestive system like the worst pain anyone could imagine. I slowly grasped my IV stand and placed my first foot unassisted on the floor. It felt like the moon landing. Next, my other leg. Pulling my once muscular, now weakened and frail figure from that bed felt like the most intense sensation anyone could imagine! I was standing by myself. *Ignore the pain....keep going, one foot in front of the other*, I thought to myself. Nothing could stop me now—no scans, no doctors, and no amount of discouraging news—because I had felt as though my body was an old holiday display that was being dismantled and disposed of after the holidays. Knocked down but not out. The desire and determination still existed.

The determination and regaining of confidence that came with rising to my feet again would motivate me in the same way a coach does his team. It all started with ignoring the pain and walking out of my room toward the nursing station at the end of the hallway. Although my epidural was still attached, I had no means to relieve the pains that were continuing to haunt me. *Grit your teeth Chuck, you are half way to the door*, I thought. Taking a brief pause and leaning at my doorway, I could eye the nursing station and the other rooms around me. It must have been three o'clock in the morning. It was a moment of great joy—I was on my way to Miami: one step, one vile, one scan at a time. The pause was short lived as I continued in my stroll across the cancer floor of the hospital. It seemed, of the dozens of patients there that day, I was the only patient that was awake celebrating 2002—the year my whole life would change physically, mentally, socially, and spiritually. Leaving the doorway, I have no idea how the strength came, but I walked the floor all the way to the nurses' station. Once there, I simply greeted them with a few laughs and a compliment. "They must have picked the prettiest nurses to work New Year's Eve...Happy New Year y'all," I said in a playful tone. Considering one was a guy, they laughed and my nurse asked what I was doing. "Trying to figure out where I can get some bubbly!" I responded. All laughed and responded that I would have to settle with some ginger ale because of my clear liquid diet. "Champagne is a clear liquid," I recall saying. "Not with your medications, Mr. Hayworth," my nurse replied. *Touché!* It would prove to be my first dose of therapy through humor. Though it certainly hurt my abs to laugh, laughter was a late yet welcome gift from 2001. It was such a somber year for our nation (and family) that I welcomed 2002 with open arms. I would open it flirting, smiling, and welcoming the road ahead to recovery.

· CHAPTER 3 ·

LET THE HEALING BEGIN

The sun was out the day I was discharged from the hospital. It was January and the gloomy days were temporarily interrupted by the sun and blue sky. After everything I had faced in that hospital, the feeling of sun on my skin and the blue sky was great! I remember a chilly breeze in the air but it was sunny and that's all that mattered! I tried insisting my folks drive toward Miami. "Come on guys, we could be there in about 12 hours and if it's this beautiful here, imagine how it looks on the beach today," I said in a confident voice, "how about Charleston, South Carolina?" I was free of the terror that was the surgical floor and would soak up every moment! No one knows what lays ahead for them.

Mom and Dad transformed their bedroom on the main level, next to our kitchen, into my temporary recovery room. It had been used for this very purpose after my Great Uncle Charles' heart surgery. It also made it easier for my mother and father to take turns keeping an eye on me until I could find the strength to make the pilgrimage up the stairs to my old room. I tried for several days, but the pain was just too intense, too daunting. Day four was the magic day when, with assistance, I could finally sleep in my own bed again, praying that I would wake up and find out this was all just a huge nightmare. That was not the case. The phone call came just a day or so later. I remember hearing the call. It was the doctor. There were subtle pauses in my mother's speech. How nightmarish it had to be for my mother to hear the word cancer used for the first time. It was determined that the tumor was a GIST Tumor; it was a slow-growing malignant tumor. Not only would my blood be monitored every day, but my cancer would be monitored by my oncologist.

My mother was my rock. She prayed for the right words to tell me. It took her two days to muster the strength to tell me everything. "It is very unusual for someone at twenty-two years old to have a GIST tumor, and to have to have it removed surgically." For now, she said I was scheduled to see a specialist. "You rest and we will talk a little more about this when you get some sleep." Her exhausted face and eyes indicated that the news would not be good. Hearing the words "you have cancer" definitely ages you instantly. I remember thinking, *I have enjoyed this life! Maybe I should ignore all of this and head for a hammock in the Keys or on an island somewhere and die with a cold drink in my hand, not a hospital bed.* The memory of my great uncle's passing from pancreatic cancer was still fresh on my mind, even though he had passed years before. Suddenly inspiration arose in my heart from folks who had struggled with this disease before. The movie quote I kept saying in my head was "get up you son of a bitch, cause Mickey loves ya," from Rocky. *Anything to keep my energy and enthusiasm high in anticipation of the long and painful road ahead*, I thought.

Since every cancer is different, so is every surgery and recovery. I would have to figure out what types of food my body could digest. Before cancer, I measured a hefty 40 waistline. Just weeks after the surgery, I was at a 32 waistline. It was an extreme weight loss, not by choice. There were countless nights of just trying to keep food down. I had hoped that no matter what I was going through, I wouldn't have to see an oncologist. And yet, my life was changed forever. To make matters worse, I had developed a blood clot in my right arm and needed to be temporarily on blood thinning shots, and eventually the medication known as Coumadin. My mom recalls, "We were dealing with numerous doctor's appointments, numerous exams, ultrasounds, constantly checking and rechecking the clot, as well as routine checks from the doctor who performed the surgery."

The morning of my first oncologist visit had arrived. I was awakened by both of my parents coming up the stairs to discuss the day ahead. This was unusual as my father was not yet retired from the practice of law. Just days earlier, I thought I was getting better and would be returning to sunny South Florida. I wanted to see our old neighbor, the only oncologist I knew. However, I was set to see a different doctor; my mother recalls that I was

adamant about not going to the appointment. I was done
seeing so many doctors! The course of my day included
visiting with my primary doctor, followed by the surgeon,
followed by the phlebotomist, and back to my surgeon for
analysis. Today was different. It was the day that I would
meet my oncologist. I really did have cancer. I could never
predict the gift of friendship being granted to me by the
great deity that beautiful, sun-filled January day. Looking
around the office, I saw members of the community and the
diversity there was in my home town. We were all unified
in our fights against cancer in spite of race, origin, religion
etc. I talked with those around me about their favorite
recipes or meals and we would all imagine the tastes and
smells which many would never have the great fortune
of eating ever again. I was still stubborn in my path to at
least taste the dishes in our imaginations as I developed
friendships with many of my fellow cancer patients
through our common love of comfort foods. Sometimes the
discussion of a simple recipe for chicken and dumplings, a
southern favorite, would cater to one's emotions and boost
the desire to beat one's cancer back. During those days,
far more folks were succumbing to cancer than are today.

The sound of children playing is not uncommon in
any doctor's office, sadly even in an oncologist office. I
remember looking at my mother square in the eyes and
she knew (even then) that I wished one day for a family,
for children of my own. At this point in my life, having just
ended a two year relationship, the desire in my heart was
to find someone who would eventually give me this gift.

It was finally time to meet my new doctor. Nothing

can describe how a moment of simple humanity could comfort me for the diagnostic tests, followed by daily blood draws, followed by office visits every other day that I would endure. I still hear his voice. "You are far too young for this. Are you sure you have the right office?" This type of therapy through humor in the doctor-patient relationship would become a major factor in my recovery. The good doctor would make many humorous remarks at my expense until one day, I felt as though we no longer had a doctor-patient relationship at all, rather two friends united in the common goal to rebuild my body and my spirit.

"Tell me your goals, Chuck," he asked.

"I want to beat cancer, Doc."

"Beyond that, what do you really want from life?"

"I want my own business, a family, a place to call my home. I want to use my skills as a chef to ensure no one has to go through this journey again like I have." Setting short term goals has been a crucial part in my recovery. It is, as I would learn from the good doctor, easier to accomplish long term goals by setting short term ones. I had one in mind—return to Miami and finish culinary school. I learned from my oncologist that this and more would be possible because I had the love and support of my friends and family. If I could give advice to anyone going through this right now, it would be to take it one step at a time. Small goals can yield big results! In my case, I was going to get better by doing something, not by standing by doing nothing. I wanted to give back but first, I needed to get better. In my case, the desires of my heart would not be sidelined by the forthcoming blood clots, or the many illnesses and problems I would have in the coming months. I could and would return to Miami in March to finish culinary school and to celebrate my birthday in April surrounded by my friends.

The road ahead would be patched full of pain and excitement, scans, and what felt like the feeding of vampires by the amount of blood that was being drawn on a daily basis. Still, I remained steadfast in my goals of returning to Miami, and finishing what I had started at all costs. It was mid-January and I had until March to be well enough to get back to school and finish my first year limping toward somewhat of a normal life again. My sickness would prove to be its own worst enemy. Deep in my heart I had just seen what my top goal was, and no one, not even the doctor had any idea what I was feeling. I wanted—more than all the luxuries of becoming a chef— to be a father and husband. I don't believe I ever informed the good doctor what his friendship has meant to me, outside of the obvious doctor-patient relationship. That day had a deep impact on my life much later as I recall it now. My focus in the immediate future was my diet and rebuilding my digestive system in my own unique way.

Every case of stomach cancer is different and requires that the patient push the boundaries a little to see what his or her digestive system can handle. Guided by my physician's advice, I had to start somewhere. My diet now consisted of yogurt, ice pops, popsicles, sports drinks, stocks, soups, noodle soups, and anything else I could drink. I found myself wondering as I would many times if I could liquefy a slice of pizza or even a burger. I began freezing exotic fruit juices because the artificial colored stuff just didn't work for me. Juicing was a new and upcoming fad, so my mother purchased any frozen fruit I desired for use in smoothies and juice shots. Flavor packets in box soup mixes became dull, so I requested help from my grandmother's fresh chicken or veggie stock. It was truly like having my own home team. Everyone was in my corner supporting my recovery. I saw more fruits and veggies in my mother's home than I had in years. If I requested mango, coconut, or any other fruit or veggie that reminded me of Florida, they made an attempt to find it at all costs. Growing up, mom always had the standard fruits around like apples, grapes, tomatoes and lemons. I introduced her to new, healing fruits and vegetables. My family's willingness to help in my recovery, no matter what it took, brought us all closer.

At this time in my recovery, I could not even think of solid foods. In all actuality, I would not dare try any until my return to culinary school. I found myself having to relearn how to taste food again. The first time I tried to eat plain white toast, I regretted it. Let's just say that sneaking this seemingly mild piece of bread would result in almost two days of the worst intestinal pains I have ever had! Everyone's body reacts to stress and change differently; this is why a nutritionist wasn't considered a medical necessity (what a mistake). In my case, eating solid food over the next three years would be difficult. The realization that a very long and complicated surgery would result in a very long and complicated recovery was beginning to set in. The solid food I consumed would seemingly ferment in my stomach. So, even after being told I could eat solid food, I remained on a liquid diet. The pains in my intestines and stomach were excruciating at times. At one point, my biggest concern was how to return to culinary school without truly tasting solid food. I didn't want any special treatments at culinary school.

· CHAPTER 4 ·

BACK TO SCHOOL

It had been three months since surgery when I decided to return to Miami, back to the life I thought was waiting for me. Although I was behind in my school work by a semester, I would be more determined than ever to complete what I had started. My parents insisted on taking a "vacation" and helped me move back to South Florida. Upon my return to school, not only had my room been given away, but almost everything I owned had been stolen or given away by my crazy roommate (who later failed out of school). Mom and Dad replaced what they could, but I still felt betrayed. I was assigned to a new room and a new set of roommates. Mom and I shopped at a large box store buying the essentials I needed. It was just the basics. One week's worth of clothes, toiletries, school uniforms, a change of sheets, and my self-setting clock radio that was given to me the previous Christmas by my grandfather. The room was a transformed condo—

two bedrooms, two bathrooms, a kitchen, a study area with cubicles and a den area which pleasantly had a cable TV belonging to one of my roommates. The owner had quarters downstairs with cats and a dog who were very friendly. She also had a dock because she lived on one of North Miami's canals. From time to time, it made for a great place to study and rest my feet in the cool water. Across the street was another dock to a man-made lake. On it was construction of another building that the school had taken over and would make into dorms the next year. It was not much, but would prove to be home. Believe it or not, I made no attempt to contact my friends on campus or off. Getting settled in was my only priority. Next stop was the grocery store. The list of essentials for living on a liquid diet in a large city would include: soup bases, electrolyte drink base, sparkling water, plain kefir, local juices, cheap local coffee, green tea, soft noodle packs, coconut milk, and soy milk. I tagged along to warehouse clubs with friends to pick up toiletries and hygiene products. Nothing could prepare me for the day I would once again walk over the bridge from the parking lot to the back door of the culinary academy. Nothing prepared me for the tremendous joy I would feel ahead. Even though I felt like I was starting over again, I had a strange suspicion that I would not be journeying alone.

I must have been greeted by at least ten people who all had similar reactions to my arrival—astonishment. Apparently, the rumor around school was that I died. I showed off my scar very proudly and explained how I would spend many days of my life in checkup offices and would jokingly ask if anyone cared to join me. My closest friends would answer the call. In order to recover and beat cancer, you need a strong support unit; one filled with friends, family and even strangers. I was happy to be back in Miami with my friends. It would be their shoulders that I would lean on. At times a laugh, a cry, a simple hug or a high five is just what you need. Amongst my friends I was never made to feel different. We all had issues in our lives, but we were all focused on the future and graduation.

It was an all-academic semester for me, no culinary labs that semester. This was essential since I was still taking the blood thinning medicines to dissolve the blood clot in my arm. One simple slice could lead to hours of unnecessary pain and suffering. In the back of my mind, I wondered how I would I keep my skills sharp. When would I be able to return to what I loved—cooking? Would I forget it all in place of academic credentials such as nutrition, economics, and basic science classes? Upon visiting with the school counselor, I was informed that this decision was made for me because of the number of doctors' appointments I would have and the risk of cutting myself while on blood thinning medications. Because of my previous college credits, I only required one semester of this prior to moving into all labs and culinary-related material.

At every opportunity, my father and mother would visit me during this semester. Dad used it as an opportunity to take CLE credits and my mother the much deserved vacation she needed for everything she went through just a few months earlier. Every time they greeted me with a hug and then my friends Jarrah and Cathy would give them a health report. These would prove invaluable. My mother steered them toward foods that I should be drinking and eating and most importantly, foods I should not be consuming. They were on the spot with these. Any time I would try solid food, I would regret it. For now, my dietary staples would be oatmeal, tofu, and heavily pulsed legumes. I do not necessarily consider those to be solid food because I always ate them in liquid form. I incorporated local avocados, Florida citruses, seasonal fruits and veggies, and of course coconuts. I could find these anywhere throughout the neighborhood. Healing myself from the land around me would become a way of life. I spent a lot of time wondering if my cancer would return and why my digestive system was healing so slowly. With every attempt to eat any type of solid food, I would throw up. This discouraged me much more than the countless hours monitoring my blood or even the scan checking for any new tumors. It was not until summer that I would attempt to try solid foods again. My mother would later recall, "when you were in Miami, you were throwing up all the time and could hardly keep food down, but then you figured out what you could eat. You figured out how to accomplish what you wanted to do with your life and become a chef."

Spring flew by and before I could sneeze, decisions needed to be made about my future course load. The advantage I had was that my university had multiple campuses that offered the classes I had missed in previous semesters. I chose Charleston, South Carolina for my summer semester. It was only four hours away from my home doctors and I could commute to my physicians and specialists in High Point! No one in Miami could understand why I would leave and spend my summer in the much smaller Charleston campus. Charleston's history could be found on every street corner. The type of cuisine was very "down home southern" and reflective of my need for healing. It would prove to be a completely different environment than Miami. Yet when one learns to taste food again, they fall in love with food again. Through observation and a great deal of maturity, I learned to literally feel romance through the "down home southern" cuisine. Its healing power would prove to heal not just my ability to taste food again, but also my spirits. It was an easy decision to go and make up the courses I had missed. The summer of healing had begun.

I learned so much while in that city. I discovered soy proteins and the importance of a daily vitamin. I discovered that I could in fact begin the long journey toward eating solid protein again. One of the most valuable courses in Charleston was my nutritional lab. I was introduced to a vegan philosophy and ingredients that would prove to be essential in my soon-to-be vegan and vegetarian life. Among these ingredients were items such as soy creams, soy milks, miso, small diced veggies, local and organic fruits and veggies that I would purée and juice. This was the summer I began my healing from the inside. Armed with the power of the importance of nourishment from the food I was able to digest, I set out with a different, more organic philosophy, one which still stays with me today. South Carolina had amazing fruits and veggies to offer.

All of the chefs, professors, and "seasoned professionals" were aware of my condition and my medical treatments, and many were not confident in my "learned" abilities from another campus. One chef even called me out in front of the class about this by trying to trick me. In one hand he held a hand full of Carolina rice called "Carolina Gold," in the other, orzo pasta. "Mr. Hayworth, can you correctly identify these two items in my hand?" It was like nothing he had ever done before. I realized that I was not as sharp as the other students in his class, but he wanted to call me out on it and prove that I needed to go back to Miami. It was the first of many times that I would be made to feel like the outsider that summer semester in the city so famous for its southern hospitality! My response was simple:

"Place those on the table, please, Chef." He did so. "Well Chef, this is orzo pasta which is commonly confused with rice because it is in a similar shape and form. This is, I believe, what y'all South Carolinians call 'Carolina Gold' rice, commonly used in rice puddings and in restaurants as risottos. Whereas orzo, being pasta, is more suited as a starch alongside grilled seafood or perhaps served chilled this time of year in a pasta salad."

I had learned so much through magazines and cookbooks at my sickest points during my recovery. Even while I was unable to hold solid food down, I was able to envision in my mind how certain dishes tasted. Reading about flavors and dishes I was still far away from trying made time go faster during my recovery. If I could not eat solid food, then I was going to train my body to envision what solid food would taste like, as well as gain knowledge of its uses and how to cook it. Out of habit, I continue to this day in my efforts writing recipes to envision flavors fused together and their tastes. Still, at every chance, the chef would try and stump my knowledge of some subtle differences in the foods we were exposed to in school. Some other questions I remember were the defining characteristics and differences between polenta and grits, broccoli versus broccolini, boiling temperatures versus poaching and simmering. My consistently correct answers led me to eventually realize that I loved all things food related to Charleston. Our game lasted throughout the semester. By the end of the class, we parted with a hand shake and a smile. With few exceptions, everything I cooked in that class was awful and bland. I would soon learn the valuable lesson of revitalizing my sense of taste by chewing the food and then spitting it out. The chef would ask how I thought I had any future in food. My response was, "by learning how to taste again, Chef." I am quite certain I was his first student with cancer, let alone stomach cancer.

After about two days of this, I met a friend who would ultimately become a close friend for many years to come. His attitude was shrewd. Thick-skinned and ever-set on achieving what he wanted made him an immediate friend. He did not buy into the university attitude which I believe was my reason for becoming friends with him right away. Adam was about five-foot-eight or so and still is the only guy that I know who makes fun of himself and everything about his family. Greer, South Carolina, his home town, was a small town just like High Point and he believed in life beyond there just as I did. We just hit it off as college buddies often do, even though some of the nutritional decisions I made when with him nearly killed me. Adam literally held me up while I was very sick from experimenting with foods. I recall him saying, "how do you know if your body can tolerate food unless you try it!" The typical "fast food" budget of a student was definitely out. None of the local restaurants except the ethnic restaurants had valuable options for me. It was a summer that neither of us would ever forget.

Summer classes were as intense as a strong cup of espresso. They were shorter than traditional classes, which meant students, including myself, had to be ready for the cramming experience. It was like taking a semester of school and cramming it into a little over a month. I would study all of the time. This included while I was waiting in any physician's office and on the weekends. While other classmates would hold regular food jobs, I would spend the time cooking for my family, learning classic styles and techniques, restaurant sanitation, and even mixology of alcoholic beverages. Not being able to taste my food, I would have to rely on my family's polite reactions.

As summer came to an end, I prayed my grades would reflect my efforts. It was also during this time that a huge announcement was made in Charleston about the university. They were closing and would only accept the next two years of enrolling students. After their graduation, the campus would move to Charlotte. "Come on y'all, make the most of it," they would say. I valued the relationships I made that summer but I did ultimately return to Miami in the fall.

It's funny how people change as time goes by. Some guys I agreed to room with off-campus showed their true colors. The party philosophy and carpe diem attitude of college was a little different for me now. There were only two more semesters and an internship standing between me and my piece of paper. Since completing all of the classes in Charleston, I found myself ahead of the game. All the classes I had left were related to Culinary Arts.

Second year students' programs were intense. French styles of service were integrated along with cuts, fabrications, and seriously difficult tastings. In my free time, I spent a large amount of time reading about food as well as driving to the different sites around the city to see with my own eyes the foods of South Florida. Whether it was a dumpling in an Asian market, or varieties of olives in an Italian market, or even the grand opening of a market I was all too familiar with, based in North Carolina. I would once again pour all of my energy into foods that I could use to heal my body from this dreadful cancer for once and for all. I still remember the day when my friend Jarrah introduced me to "miso soup." Locally grown, smashed plantains and sweet potatoes were a part of my new semi-liquid, semi-solid diet. I began thinking, *maybe I could slowly and gradually add solid foods back into my diet*. This was much harder than I thought it would be. Healing takes time but I was growing impatient. I had gone from being an extra-large and husky figure, a perception that most Americans thought at the time would make for a great chef, to a much smaller size. Needless to say, I wanted relief from my liquid diet; I wanted to eat solid food again. I spent countless days vomiting or with food fermenting in my stomach. Weeks passed by and still I longed for some sense of a normal diet. The world was at war with terrorism, and I was fighting a war within myself. I would never again take for granted what nourishment solid food could give.

In class, I would simply excuse myself to the men's restroom and lose all that I had to eat, even the liquids, but at least I tasted my cooking. This would become my attitude. I had arrived back in Miami stronger than before and much more determined. I would not allow myself to be distracted or discouraged by my sarcastic classmates or my harsh instructors.

Next, I wanted to hold some type of job. I responded to a posting I found around campus for a temp agency and decided to do some temp work around Miami for some spending money. This helped me tremendously and also helped pad the resume with some solid experience prior to my internship interviews with major hotels and resorts. My assignments included contract events around town including cooking for awards ceremonies and even motion picture production companies. Call it fate or destiny, my internship the following semester would be at the most popular Central Florida family destination. I spent the winter of 2002 in Central Florida with the most unlikely of people—my brother Mike. As it turns out, he had spent the previous summer working an internship with this resort while I was in Charleston and was eligible for rehire. I think he was, in his own way, keeping an eye on me for Mom because this would be the first holiday season away from home for both of us.

This internship provided many opportunities for college students. The orientation lasted three days, one of which was a full introduction to the do's and don'ts with company protocol. It was here that I would have to learn not only how to balance my anxiety and health problems, but also my cooking abilities and social abilities. This place had long been a desired location for college interns because of the legendary parties that were thrown to blow off steam! Yet I was not there to party, only to get well and learn a few things. My brother helped me settle into the life of an intern in Central Florida. He kept a close eye on my health. We were assigned work at the same restaurant; he would entertain, and I would cook. I felt honored to work alongside the many industry veterans for breakfast, lunch, and dinner shifts.

Among the new ingredients to which I was exposed were Israeli couscous, Swiss chard, house-smoked salmon, yams, and watercress to name just a few. Many of these proved to be key components in an organic, local, vegan, ground-up approach to recovering from stomach cancer. My family broke tradition and spent the week before Christmas in a hotel on the property. It was a great time for all of us. We were able to get the family some serious discounts as interns. Even my older brother, Joe, joined us from Jacksonville. We celebrated my grandparents' 50th wedding anniversary as well as the holidays together. I don't think anyone thought we would be celebrating this way a year ago.

A new year, 2003, was approaching and with its arrival came many things: hope of beating the dreadful disease of cancer, hope of graduation, and hope of the life to come. Although I would welcome it with total strangers from behind a food line in this resort, my brother was here with me, a piece of home, and the memory stays with me. I cried that evening like I never had before. Excusing myself to the walk-in cooler, leaning against the chilled shelves of food, I burst out into tears of joy and sadness, pain and relief. Feeling as though hell was beyond me, ready to take on the world, I returned to the chef yelling orders in my face wondering where the hell I had been! It would prove to be the last confrontation I would have with a chef of any type. I shrugged it off and went back to work. Only a few more weeks, and this, too, would be over. The memories and friendships created here would last a lifetime. Another short-term goal was met—I ushered in another year.

Fueled by the new year, I found new energy and confidence from within. Just a year ago I was in a hospital bed, and now I was on my way to accomplishing another goal. It had been a tough year considering all the pain, countless hours of visits to multiple doctors' offices, procedures, and many discouraging thoughts. With the start of 2003, I promised myself a better year—a year of setting goals and keeping to them. Baby steps and realistic goals were the way, just as I had been advised by my oncologist. It was time! Reenergized by the new year ahead, I put everything behind me and returned to Miami, ready to finish strong.

· CHAPTER 5 ·

GRADUATION, CHARLESTON & AILEEN

I began my final semester on a rainy Monday in March. During the semester, I was still weak and though my doctors and parents advised me not to work, I called the agency from time to time. Some truly amazing opportunities came my way, including working for award ceremonies and several motion picture companies. It was stressful but rewarding and a great experience. At this time, I became closer friends with the man I nicknamed Uncle Walt, a retired airline pilot and war veteran. He, too, was a cancer survivor. We kept great company together and developed recipes around our common love of food.

In April, my friend Adam called me to let me know that the Charleston campus was accepting transfer students until the summer semester. This seemed like an odd time for a change as graduation was quickly approaching and my only focus was on graduating from culinary school.

After much thought, I committed to another summer in Charleston after graduation.

Graduation was over Memorial Day weekend. I remember it well because Miami held its second annual Urban Beach Week in South Beach that same weekend. Being a holiday weekend, my entire family including my grandparents decided to come down on Thursday. I remember trying to make reservations all over town and all the restaurants were booked. I wanted my family to see the culture of South Florida! The beauty of South Beach was the allure of the beaches, the restaurants, and the people. This was the reason I was so attracted to this place. Since everywhere was full, my family had to stay in Broward County, much farther north than they had expected.

Dad had developed a tradition of falling asleep at various graduations since high school; this tradition was broken with a speech by the CEO of Carnival Cruise Lines. The CEO spoke that sweltering day about the future of the industry. It was funny to see that he nodded off a bit, but did not fall asleep. An ongoing joke between us was that if I were to live in South Florida, he was determined to look like Hemmingway, and so, he grew his beard. Mike and Dad purchased some "local" cigars for the occasion. When I stepped foot on stage to receive my associate's degree, my cheering section began to get quite loud. I wanted to leap out of my skin. I did it! Another major goal was accomplished!

I returned to Charleston, only a few hours away from my home doctors to complete my bachelor's degree requirements for the summer, and perhaps return to Miami in the fall. I had interviewed for a seasonal chef position in a major Charleston-area resort, and the job was mine, provided I committed to staying in Charleston for the summer. This felt right. This time I could hold my head high and make a new home for myself. This time in Charleston, I would feel like a normal student, not an outsider as before. I found that the key to transferring to another campus was enrolling in summer courses and just deciding to stay for the following semester.

It is funny how when you least expect it you are sent the one and only love of your life. Charleston had proven to be my Rome as Miami had been my Paris, but little did I know that a romance beyond learning to taste food in an exciting, new way would blossom this time. Just as Rome was one of most historic cities in Europe, Charleston was the oldest city in The Carolinas. The origin of romance is Rome, and Charleston would be the city in which I would fall in love for the first time ever. It was this summer season that I would fall in love with food and cooking as well as my soulmate, Aileen.

Everything I owned was in my 1998 Jeep Wrangler on its way up I-95 from Miami to Charleston when I received a call on my cell phone. My mother called to ask me if I would escort my old friend Allison to her brother's rehearsal dinner that weekend. I agreed to do the favor. I drove past Charleston and directly to Chapel Hill, North Carolina where my mother greeted me with a room key and a suit bag. After about twenty minutes of cleaning up and settling into my hotel room, there was a knock on the door. It was my mother explaining that the guests for the rehearsal dinner were already downstairs, and that I should follow her down. Met by Allison, my date for the evening, I remember seeing so many people who congratulated me on my graduation and joked about the food and me. This evening would prove to be an evening of memories. Not only did I meet my future wife, but it was the first time in a long time that I would be able to eat and actually digest solid foods. Maybe it was the menu (the food was high in ginger and garlic) or maybe it was the company; no matter what, I felt great. We would be seated at the table of love, the singles' table.

Before dinner, I saw Aileen from across the room, and the new confident Chuck asked Allison who she was. Before I knew it, Aileen was heading our way to confirm Allison was indeed the groom's sister (it had been years since the two had seen each other) and wondering who I was. "Just an old friend of Allison's," I responded, introducing myself. Aileen was all I could ever have dreamed of and more! But she was way out of my league. Aileen was the head of Human Resources for a local community bank in Raleigh. She and I hit it off right away, and I knew that we had a spark. Later that evening, after a lot of laughing and flirting, Aileen asked to see my ID because she did not believe my age. I explained that I was a recent culinary school graduate from Miami now living in Charleston. She told me about the years she spent in Miami. I tried impressing her with my work with celebrities, but it was food that linked us. They say that when you truly feel love for the first time it bowls you over. That evening, Aileen and I were inseparable. Our common love for all things food and wine led to an evening of many memories which we still discuss and celebrate to this day. One of the last things Aileen said that night was that she had never been to Charleston. So, I insisted she come and visit. She did and the rest is history—our history! Allison saw the chemistry between Aileen and me that night as though we were ignoring her. The truth was, that night I had a spark lit within me which I had never felt before.

The following week while I was in High Point for my checkups, Allison called wondering if I would be willing to take her down to see Aileen and her roommate in Durham. "Are they expecting me?" I asked Allison. She just laughed it off and insisted that since Aileen and I had hit it off at the wedding, it seemed like a good opportunity to see this remarkable woman— whom it seemed I had known for a lifetime—again. It was that weekend that I opened my heart and told her everything about my illness and my journey toward recovery. I offered no guarantees that I would be living in a year (it was like a bad pick up line), but I highlighted the reality of my life, which had proved to be too much for her predecessor.

That night, we released all of our "baggage" in a simple series of questions and answers which lasted until the early morning. All I needed to do now was slowly "unharden" her heart, so to speak. Simply walking her two dogs around the pond of her apartment complex would solidify an ongoing bond of love and support which lasts to this day. There were three gazebos around the pond. At each, I posed a question to her. I asked the first question:

"If by the end of the summer things are still going the way they are with us, would you be willing to be in an exclusive relationship with me?" Pausing for what seemed like an eternity, she responded with one simple word: "sure." That was not good enough for me. I had never met someone so amazingly beautiful with whom I had so much in common. Perhaps I could use all the confidence I had and could possibly muster up! I had to change her mind about dating a younger guy by the end of this walk. It was like a chess match. *Check!* We would both use sneaky descriptions and hint at how our heart had been broken the entire walk. I could tell that her heart had been broken and indeed she had volunteered this to me, but at this point, I had to have her as mine. Pausing at the second gazebo, just a slightly different question: "So if things are proceeding as they are now between us, do you think that by the end of the month you may be willing to be in an exclusive relationship with me?" My stomach was in my throat. Keep in mind that I was a student and a cancer patient. That's a lot for a young professional in her late twenties to take on. This time she would simply let out a flirtatious smile and a nod of her head. From this point, I had to go for the "full monty" and lay it all on the line! If she was willing to take on a culinary graduate working on a higher degree and a cancer patient, here was the real test. With all my might as we began to walk the short distance to the last gazebo, I let out a sigh and went for it all: "How about by the end of the weekend?" She responded with the same flirtatious smile, "ok, that sounds about right." Wow! As we arrived at her apartment, I realized that that too was not good enough! "Aileen, I want you and you alone. I know I am a student and a cancer patient. I know I am not the ideal match you had envisioned, but I….think I …um I must have you as mine. I have to have you as my girlfriend and potentially more." Then I asked one last simple question knowing that we were meant to be together: "What if I was 30 and not 23, what would you say to me then?" She said she would ask where her ring was! That heart of hers was melted with a kiss from me at that doorstep those many years ago. With that kiss, I became more confident than ever that no matter what was ahead of me with my health, my journey would never again be a lonesome one. I had her shoulder to lean on through thick and thin and she accepted me for who I was despite knowing the odds. For that and many other things, I have pledged my heart to her forever.

Just days later, I reported to my first job as a culinary graduate and moved into university housing, with my old pal, Adam, as a roommate. Somehow I was able to juggle part-time classes at the university, medical appointments, working in the kitchen and a new relationship all at once. As it turned out, my new job would be a seasonal position with a major golf resort in Charleston which generated just enough savings for me to purchase a diamond engagement ring for this extraordinary woman. I asked her jokingly to describe her ideal wedding and engagement ring, and it would take only weeks to find it.

That summer, I truly had a muse in Aileen which provided the much desired incentive to master how to taste food again. Aileen recalled that "six weeks into our relationship, eating at a five star hotel's restaurant in Charleston for Bastille Day would be my first indication of how sick you were." I later informed her of my strong desire to introduce her to the wonderful flavors of this city despite the crushing blow the "down home southern" style cuisine would give to my health. It was a once-in-a-lifetime opportunity to fall in love in what I saw as the greatest city in the South. During the early days of our relationship, I wanted to impress her with my knowledge of what it was like to learn to taste food for the first time again. This was achieved, oftentimes at the expense of my health. Nevertheless, convincing Aileen that I would be able to provide for her took a lot more than just the occasional night on the town. I would have to make big and dramatic moves if I was to truly win her. It was time to move out of student housing and into my own place.

The hardest part about being a student and courting someone like Aileen, a professional human resource officer, was feeling like I had to find the perfect apartment that was central to everything great in Charleston. In those days, affordable housing didn't really exist for students in downtown Charleston. I settled for a small studio apartment which she would describe as "smelling like Charleston." Just as Rome has an appreciation for historical cultures, so did Charleston. The apartment had a distinct musty smell, a small galley kitchen with four burners, and a seemingly small oven which could barely fit any dish I used. Only inches from the oven stood a counter with a sink, and to my delight, a tiny dishwasher. Right next to my stove was my far-too-small refrigerator.

Outside of the kitchen area was a counter that I would use as my combination dining room/office. Protruding from the wall next to that was a Murphy bed with a closet housing my hot water heater. Next to the closet was my bathroom, surprisingly equipped with a full shower and tub and a pitiful sink with mirror. I remember thinking, *is she going to like this place?* It was all I could afford. She was all I cared about. Off my balcony, I could see King Street in the distance, the shopping and fashion district in Charleston. The studio wound up being perfect for me and for us. Its proximity not only to King Street, but The Charleston Market, Rainbow Row, The Battery, and especially Meeting Street–where artists, musicians, university life, and the festival known as "Spoleto" join together at a central point called Marion Square—was ideal. With this as our backdrop, it would make falling in love an experience we both would not soon forget. Aileen describes Charleston as "the city where she truly fell in love with me." She proved to be the missing piece of the equation; she kept my eating habits on track. Being alone during the first year after surgery had proven to be a long road, but I was no longer alone on my path towards recovery. She would accept the many faults I carried with me during this tedious path of recovery. She would be the much-needed muse to prove I still could follow my chosen career path of becoming a professional chef. Walking the streets of Charleston as a couple sealed a bond of love and romance which was especially prevalent in the organic markets. For the first time, I had a reason to continue with the healing process. Through her love and affection, I would find a spark for healing which had, up to that point, been long lost. She was the chief reason for my healing through nourishment of organic, natural, and local foods.

The romantic summer flew by as most do. Fall was approaching and I would be a full-time student with a new goal: to purchase that ring and ask Aileen to marry me. She and I knew by this point that it was far more than a summer fling, but rather true love. I remember finally having enough money to purchase the ring of her dreams. I remember the driving determination with every cut, bruise, and burn, which brought me to that moment. I was so excited I could have screamed. Instead, I listened to a musical melody of tunes that she and I had always enjoyed as I made the four-hour trip up the interstate highway to Raleigh from Charleston.

· CHAPTER 6 ·

MEETING HER FAMILY

No self-respecting southern man would even think of asking for a woman's hand without the consent of the men in her life. In Aileen's case, I would have to travel to the Caribbean island of Puerto Rico to make this happen. Her family was well aware of who I was and how I had come into her life by now, but had yet to meet me. We were three months into our relationship when Aileen and I decided to attend her grandfather's birthday party in Puerto Rico. We would surprise my future in-laws with my arrival for the festivities. The only person in her family with any knowledge of my arrival was her mother. It was the ideal situation to get to know her family as she had mine during the summer months. The flight was awful; we were delayed for hours in Miami (on the tarmac) due to a bad storm. I asked her to tell me all about the family members I would meet and all of the sights I would be able to see in my inaugural trip to Puerto Rico. The delay forced us to reveal the surprise to her family, in particular her father, that it would be Aileen plus one for the festivities. Expecting anger, I was pleasantly surprised that his only concern was the already immaculate condition of his home, appearing to be even more magazine ready for the new "man" in Aileen's life.

When we finally arrived in San Juan, I recall Aileen requesting a *malupina* from her Dad. This was a drink which I learned she had created in past trips with friends consisting of coconut rum and fresh pineapple juice. As our ride pulled up to the curb, I was amazed to find an entire van full of her family—they had all come to meet us at the airport. Out of the front seat rushed her father to help me load the luggage.

"It's nice to meet you sir. I am Chuck Hayworth."

"You too. I'm Roy. Let's book it. We have to beat the traffic." A reaction of laughter, which words cannot describe, came from the back seat. It was her grandmother and grandfather. As it turned out, her grandmother had been at the hairdresser last minute in order to make a positive impression on the "new guy." A barrage of questions headed my way: *Is this your first trip to Puerto Rico? Have you traveled much? Where is your family from in North Carolina?* I responded to these and more. Since I had been in an airplane for the majority of the day, I had a vision of jumping in a pool somewhere. Almost as if we were on the same page, her grandfather, who was already in a swimsuit, asked me if I liked swimming.

"I could definitely take a dip", I said.

"Aileen did not tell you we have a pool?" He asked,

surprised. I was sure at some point she had, but I was so engulfed in the moment. It was all so surreal. I was meeting my future in-laws and finding out if the Spanish I had learned in Miami was enough to keep up with all of the conversation. Yet, to my surprise, they all spoke English. As we pulled into the driveway of their Guaynabo residence, my heart was beating out of my chest. I remember thinking I would have to wait for an opening. I would have to wait until something would bring the subject of marriage up. Meeting this family in these few moments had proven more intimidating than any lecture from a "seasoned chef". No sooner had the car had been placed in park than her grandfather hopped out as if he were a child and cannonballed into the oasis that was a pool in my future father-in-law's backyard. I was given a dime tour and told by her grandfather to put my swim trunks on and to come in the pool. I settled into my temporary guest room, the office couch, and headed to the pool. This would become a place I would refer to as my "office" while I was visiting them. Still, my nerves were not as calm as they should have been due to the silence of my future father-in-law, Roy.

As if I had been sent a gift from above, I would finally prove my worth early the next morning during a time of emergency. As it turned out, the hallway bathroom sink had leaked all over the house in the middle of the night. I was awakened by Aileen explaining to me to be careful with all of the wires which were on the floor of the office. There must have been at least a half-inch or more of water on the floor. We grabbed any and all mops, brooms, and towels and jumped into action. Even the neighbors were bringing squeegees and brushes over, anything that could rid the house of the ever deepening water. Eventually her grandfather, ever the handyman, switched the water off. Everyone sprang into action to get all of the water out of the house. I had been in my pajama pants and tee-shirt through all of this. We didn't stop until all of the water was out of the house. All morning and slightly into the afternoon, we swept the water out of the house. It was the perfect moment to see, with my persistence, if I might be able to bring up marrying Aileen.

"Well, now that that's finished, I would really like to talk with you about marrying your daughter." I finally said.

"You are a full time student," he responded.

"I am almost through with school, and really want to start my own business. My family has always been self-employed," I told him. He asked me what my father and mother did for a living. Then the question which every man who is doing this properly hears: "How do you plan to provide for her?"

With my throat in my stomach, I responded with, "I hope to start my own catering and restaurant business someday. I promise you will receive a phone call first when I wish to make it official." I suppose after all we had just been through, I had won his respect at that point. I explained how my cancer had changed my whole outlook on cooking for a living. When I started college, my strongest desire was corporate advancement. By this point, I wanted to provide a life for his daughter. What I did not mention to him was my desire to have a family as well. A simple faucet leak that flooded the home brought the two of us together and has served as a reminder to us of what type of relationship we would have together as father and son. I knew right then and there that he had given his blessings, but would not make it official until a ring was purchased. I would now have to win the hearts and minds of the rest of her family in Puerto Rico in a different way.

One afternoon, after the flood, we headed to the residence of her grandparents who lived on the island. Having already won the hearts of her other grandparents and her father, I could not meet her other grandparents empty-handed. We stopped at a roadside produce stand, which was near where her grandparents lived, and picked up the biggest, ripest, juiciest pineapple I could find. As we entered the neighborhood, I remember feeling comfortable and relaxed. Recalling my Spanish, I would chime in where I could in conversation. The building was constructed of solid concrete, as were many buildings in Puerto Rico, to withstand possible hurricane damage. Her grandmother and grandfather lived on the lower level and her aunt on the top level. Around back was a private rental entrance which they used for additional income. It was home to Aileen many summers growing up, and I had eagerly anticipated seeing the pictures and records of Aileen's youth that her grandparents held so dearly. Walking up a small stone path to a gated outdoor porch, I saw someone who could only be her *abuelo* resting in a far corner hammock, as a cool breeze passed through the breezeway. I presented him with the pineapple and the

words, "mucho gusto a usted. Me llamo Chuck," to which
Roy added, in Spanish, that I had made him help select
this pineapple so I did not arrive empty-handed. The
smile on Aileen's grandfather's face beamed, and it's that
same smile that I think of during dark wintery days. That
type of happiness is contagious. The following evening, we
celebrated her grandfather's birthday, and before I knew
it, it was time for us to return to our daily lives; Aileen to
the bank and me to school to start fall classes.

When I arrived in Raleigh several weeks after
our trip to Puerto Rico, my heart was beating out of
my chest and I had not yet even purchased the ring.
It was one of those life-changing moments that a man
should remember when he falls into difficult times in his
marriage. I had planned on meeting Aileen for lunch.
I left Charleston earlier telling her I would be in High
Point for my appointments, but instead I spent that time
across the street from her office in Raleigh at the mall
purchasing what would be the perfect engagement ring
for her. The excitement of the day was written all over
my face. I found it, would have it sized correctly, then
find the right moment, the perfect, unexpected moment
and ask the question. I remember thinking, *who should
I tell about this first? Who will pick up their phone first?*
I called my older brother, Joe, first. Always cautious
since learning of my cancer, Joe lacked the celebratory
response I had expected, and responded by asking, "are
you sure this is what you want to do? Is she even aware
of how sick you are? Why would she want to take on that
type of responsibility? God forbid your cancer recovery

takes a bad turn." I ended the call with "thanks for caring, Joe," and in a simple sarcastic tone, "I will talk with you later, goodbye."

Hoping my mother's reaction would be a little different, I paused and dialed. "Mom, I bought a ring for Aileen and plan on asking her to marry me." All she cared about was the details of how I had purchased it and its looks and certifications, etc. Unlike Joe, she congratulated me and wished us well. My mother had gotten to know Aileen very well during the summer; the two of them accompanied me to the overwhelming number of doctor appointments for which I returned to High Point. Her feelings about her future daughter-in-law were settled that summer the first time Aileen had visited her home with flowers and a bottle of wine. Later that summer, Aileen would be by my mother's side in Aileen's home as the two of them would carry my weakened body off of the floor of her cold guest bathroom where I had just thrown up. Together, they would help to clean me up and escort me to the base of Aileen's bed. The three of us have been through so much, which still provides strength to our relationship.

Finally, the moment had arrived. It was time to call Roy and make it official. I called the house and my future mother-in-law answered. I explained the great news and she informed me that Roy was in the air headed to St. Croix on business. She would have him call me, knowing now what I had done. When we finally spoke, I told him, "I just could not wait. I had to buy your daughter an engagement ring. Do I have your blessing to proceed?" He responded, "of course Chuck." All I had to do now was graduate and head to Raleigh to find employment. The ring would be available and sized two days later. I then called her best friend, her roommate, her brother, and another close friend and asked them as well. When the ring was ready, I asked her in the most unlikely of ways. I had informed her that I would be taking her to a nice restaurant for dinner and that I had something very special to discuss with her. Instead of waiting until dinner, I got down on one knee and asked her to marry me in her casual game-day attire. She teared up, and explained how the ring was perfect. I responded with a simple, "I love you. I think we can go to dinner now, so I am going to take a shower." I never regretted not waiting until dinner to ask her to marry me.

Many college students have told me horror stories of their final few semesters. The work load becomes more and more intense with exams and tests around every corner. I don't look back at my final semesters in college as being that challenging, but rather the opposite. Up to this point, I had been through so much more than the challenges my final semester held for me. It was far more difficult to learn to eat solid foods again than it was tackling my senior seminar, for example. I would pour all of my efforts into creating impressions and reading and learning as much as I possibly could about this industry with the goal of someday having a life free from scheduling around doctor visits. I took accounting classes, followed by statistics, followed by senior seminar, where I would present all that I had learned in the form of case studies from hospitality companies where I had been employed over the years. Aileen provided the much-needed inspiration, and at times the love and support I needed to make it all the way to graduation.

All my hard work with her help was enough to earn me cum laude distinctions at graduation that summer. I had officially marked off of my list the goal which the previous graduation had only given me half of—a four-year college degree. The support of family, friends, and of course my now fiancée, Aileen, had been a blessing through my arduous journey toward having a college degree. Graduation was held on the campus of The Citadel, a beautiful military college in Charleston. I remember, upon being issued my cap and gown, finding myself in a moment of great humility. *What will I do with my life to provide for Aileen? What if my cancer returns?* Putting aside the negative feelings, I found a white piece of chalk which many were using to write messages on their caps, and inscribed a message for all to read: *Not Even Cancer*. These three words would bring comfort to me in the years to come. They would serve as a reminder that *not even cancer* could bring me down from the cloud I was on during that moment. I had seen so many dark and dreary moments to get to this point. I had a bachelor's degree from one of the top culinary and hospitality schools in the country. It was up to me to use what I had learned to make a difference in the lives of those around me.

· CHAPTER 7 ·

THE WEDDING

In October, right before our wedding, I took a job at a private club in Raleigh. When I was hired, I explained to the manager that I would need two weeks off for my wedding in Puerto Rico and our honeymoon. He was an exciting, jovial, and loving type of manager. I could tell in his case that he had worked his way up the ladder with the school of hard knocks. He and I had a common love for great wines and how they paired with food, a trait I was slowly picking up with Aileen by my side. I would have to because our honeymoon was in Napa Valley, California. This was a dream destination. Time flew by, and before I knew it my title was Banquet Captain. I was in charge of overseeing all of the banquet staff in the club. Many former coworkers would describe me as being the "stressed-out" manager. I was at any given point planning a wedding while at the same time coordinating other events for brides and grooms. I also had to work late hours in some cases until 3:00 AM. In contrast, Aileen was working bank hours. The departure week had finally come. I was leaving the club for two weeks—my wedding and honeymoon.

The ceremony was held under an archway at the most elegant hotel and resort in San Juan. We were married by my grandfather in the tropical setting of Puerto Rico. It was followed by a cocktail hour and finally a fabulous dinner. Aileen and I had planned every detail, especially the food for both the rehearsal dinner and the wedding. Our families made the plans come true. Over time, I look back at it as being a great and monumental occasion for me in my health as well. From that day forward, I have confessed my love to Aileen. She was like a princess floating across the dance floor with our first dance. These moments feel like they come and go far too quickly. At times I have found myself wishing I could rewind time and dance once more, free of all the worries and cares in the world.

The day following the wedding, we flew from San Juan to Miami, Miami to Charlotte, and finally Charlotte to San Francisco. I was incredibly tired in Charlotte, and by the time we landed in San Francisco, I couldn't even see straight. Something was terribly wrong but I had no idea what it was. I was beyond exhausted yet insisted that Aileen drive our tiny rental car from the airport to the wine country. All I remember thinking was, *do not scare her. I know I am sick and I have no idea what is wrong. Should I tell her?* All I could mutter was, "wow, I am exhausted. We just flew from the Caribbean to California in one day." What was Mother Nature throwing my way now? I could barely stay awake until I smelled something so distinct—it was harvest time! We had arrived at the outskirts of wine country. It was one of the most beautiful regions I had ever seen. My expectations of Napa were completely wrong. It had a much smaller town feel than I think Aileen or I had expected. Aileen would be dealt her first case of my illness the following day.

She and I had planned to spend half of our honeymoon in Napa and the other half in San Francisco. I remember feeling exhausted, even after a whole evening of solid sleep. We were scheduled to have a couple's massage when I felt weak and chilly. My massage would end abruptly with me having to soak my whole body in the hottest water possible for almost an hour. I just couldn't get warmed up. I never knew the cause of this; however it weakened me for nearly two entire days. As she had many times before, Aileen simply stayed by my side and comforted me. All of the change in my life coming so swiftly, coupled with my body finally relaxing from the nightmare it had been through with my cancer, in all likelihood led to a complete restart. Reflecting back on it, Aileen always says the same thing: "I know Papa said in sickness and in health, but I had no idea it would be tested so quickly!"

As a result of the days lost in bed, we both decided to stay in Napa instead of heading to San Francisco. We also agreed to see my physician in High Point when we returned. I felt sick the entire trip but I tried to disguise my illness through each and every tasting. I was determined to make the most of our trip to Napa. It was as though I were tasting food and wine for the first time again.

Admittedly, this trip would be much more to me than just a honeymoon.

Our room faced a well-known port producers vineyard. Each morning, we would wake to the sights and sounds of the vineyard. Seeing the dew on grape leaves as the sun rose over the vineyard is a sight I often recall during stressful times. The heavenly scent of the autumn roses mixed with the smell of the toasted oak barrels. As a farmer would describe it to me, "one vintage down; now it's time to work on the next harvest." Growing anything takes this type of effort, especially grapes. It was amazing to see this every day up close. Back east, we could only marvel at the bottle and dissect its flavor, but here we were witnessing the birth of a new vintage. It represented far more than just the birth of a marriage; it would provide me with inspiration that all would be well with this extraordinary woman, who I now called my wife, by my side. We saw Napa as the natives did, one grocery store meal at a time. Simple food such as a rotisserie chicken with sautéed broccolini and a great bottle of wine, for example, are what we still reminisce about. Before we knew it, it was time for us to return to the daily grind.

· CHAPTER 8 ·

MY LIFE IS FOREVER CHANGED

It proved to be a rocky return to the club. My once jovial boss had been promoted to a new position in the "sister" club. He was replaced by the former manager of the main dining room who was the type of manager who must always be in control of everything. To make matters worse, his micromanaging tactics were constantly undermining the foothold I was trying to achieve with my staff. Over time, it proved to be much more than I could handle. I had to make a decision about the future of my career. Countless meetings with management and with him would result in my decision to look for another position within the company. In the end, I opted for working on the line in the main dining room for several months while interviewing for a new position elsewhere. During my time with the club, Raleigh saw one of the worst winter storms in its history. It was also during this time that I would have my first cancer scare in my new marriage.

I was learning that the stress from my job combined with managing my illness and a new marriage would prove to be too much. On the day after Thanksgiving, about 4 weeks after our wedding, I found a lump that scared us both. Aileen then uttered the most magnificent words that would change my life forever. "If I cannot have you, then I will have a piece of you." She was determined to start a family at that very minute, "just in case." I felt helpless. I had to find a way to overcome the fear of possible return of my cancer. Aileen and I would also decide together that I would have to resign. Weeks would pass until it was determined to be a false alarm. The cancer had not returned, but I was starting a life in a more family-friendly kitchen—university dining.

University dining at one of our state's largest universities placed me back in the kitchen where I belonged with the title of sous-chef. My strongest desire was to be in sales, but with a lack of experience in this arena, I was placed in the kitchen. I was finally in a position where my hours were more similar to Aileen's. It was a dream come true. Aileen told me during this time period that she was pregnant. I approached my boss about moving from my kitchen and interviewing for a management position within another kitchen, in a well-known private university. It, at first, seemed to be a dream assignment.

Everyone in this kitchen was impressed with the kitchens I had worked at or run. It was my attitude that would land my production manager position in this very large kitchen. I would soon discover that the kitchen was packed with union employees. It was here that I learned the corporate chain of command. Running this kitchen gave me a good perspective on how companies, at the time, were running quite large labor budgets. Looking back, I was not sure who I was directly reporting to, causing confusion every time an issue would come up, which was nearly daily. I was handed a group of cooks who had been performing the same duties, in some cases, for over thirty years. It was never clearly outlined to me that as the production manager I was not to cook under any circumstances. Of course, one exception to this existed— showing a unionized cook how to properly cook an item. I was responsible for performing the duties of many, but was only one person. Every week, the union rep would file a grievance against me, and I would wind up in my boss's office. Aileen and I played a game called "How Many Grievances" because oftentimes in this job I was grieved multiple times during the day. I joked that I would never see my new child because I was working on grievances. In my heart my deepest desire was to help these cooks learn something every day. They would even call me on my days off with questions about the dishes we had been making together for months. I took it all with stride. A great majority of these workers were doing exactly what I was, trying to save as much as they could for the next generation to have a better life.

So many people recall the birth of their first child as being life-altering. I was just scared as hell. All I remember is Aileen trying so hard to give birth naturally. She and I arrived at the hospital in Raleigh the day before, only to be turned away after a few hours because she was not dilated enough. "We are in this together sweetheart. I am here for you." I was starving, and we decided with my parents to head to dinner for a little while. She was in labor, craving a shrimp and arugula pizza from our favorite spot near the hospital. We routinely went there after taking the parenting classes sponsored by the hospital. She painfully took breaths. The server would ask how she was, and Aileen will always laugh at my mother's response. Mom said very nonchalantly to the server, "she is just in labor, she's fine."

"Just in labor" would prove to be a little more serious than we thought.

After what Aileen would explain as being an "excruciatingly painful" dinner, we went home. The next day, everything was different. This was definitely the day! The biggest day of our lives had arrived. Aileen was with my parents when I left for work. I could not stay and help her cope with labor until I made sure that all management and kitchen staff were on the same page. I had filed the necessary paperwork with management and worked six hours until I checked in with Aileen. She informed me she was truly in labor but was luckily with my parents. I thanked the cooks for all their hard work and explained that the office manager would be in the kitchen while I was out for family leave. I also explained how my wife was now in labor, and was shocked at the many congratulatory words from my kitchen employees.

When I arrived home, Aileen and my mother were keeping track of her contractions, but now it was time to get to the hospital. Scared cannot even come close to what we would face next. I had avoided an operating room since having the tumor taken out and would have to remain strong for the both of us. It was the first sign of fear on Aileen's face I had ever seen. The umbilical cord was wrapped around the baby's neck and he had to come out. To make matters worse, they rushed her out of the room before we could speak to each other. Panic had set in. I yelled, "I'll see you in the operating room!"

I was escorted down a long cold hallway where I was shown where to change into scrubs. The nurse who had escorted me to this room told me to wait until I was asked to join them in the operating room. I was just praying to have the strength. Not long after I had gotten changed into scrubs, as if I could feel her fear, I yelled to Aileen from a distance, "don't be afraid!"

Emerson came into the world shortly after I was escorted in the operating room. "How are you Aileen? Are you ok?" I swore I would never return to an operating room, and yet there I stood. I was escorted to a room which I have since called a "cleaning room." This is the room where they clean the babies before handing them to the husband or partner prior to letting the mother hold the baby. The sound of a baby crying for the first time is truly an amazing feeling. After cleaning the baby I was informed by the nurse that "this is the time to share the baby with mommy." Aileen's smile that day was enough to comfort any discouragement I had. "Here he is, this is Emerson." I was then ushered out and placed in a room awaiting my beautiful wife and child. Ever mindful of my desire to start my own business at some point in the future, my mind wondered, *how will I provide for him on a salary that barely pays the bills?* I remember talking with my father that week about starting my business and his saying that he would consult on any legal needs. The seed was planted.

Days after returning home from the hospital, Aileen's incision became infected. It was our first anniversary and she couldn't get out of bed without shaking. Something was terribly wrong. We headed to the emergency room, but left once they started handing out pillows since there were no beds available. She made an appointment for 9 o'clock the next morning. I went to work and she went to the doctor with her mother and the baby. The infection was much worse than even the doctor expected. She needed a second surgery to remove all the infected tissue. I have always felt that the infection was caused by the doctor's error.

Because of how the system was structured at the time, our medical insurance would not cover home healthcare of her wound. I remained calm and had to spend a week on the seventh floor of the hospital in Raleigh, commuting nearly forty-five minutes to work every day. A simple pump machine was keeping Aileen's body clean from infection. I thought I knew what scared looked like. She was in the hospital for two days and crying because she did not have her baby. We had hoped to keep the baby away from hospital germs but we had to do it. We would be a family no matter what was thrown our way. The tides had turned on me. It was my turn to take care of her during the course of her recovery as she had me. I had to balance work with family time and place my own health on the back burner. Lack of sleep coupled with the stress of the unionized kitchen and a difficult office environment finally caught up with me one day when my boss began to criticize me. It became overwhelming for my health to constantly deal with this bombardment. I loved my job, but the pains in my stomach, symptomatic of possible ulcers, coupled with serious headaches was becoming too much for my system to handle.

"Where were you on the 17th of this past month? I have a record of the union trying to page you with issues all week that week," he asserted.

"I was in the hospital with my wife giving birth to my child," I responded.

"You were supposed to be on call. I have no record of you checking in."

I responded confidently with, "Check with your cooks. They knew that I had left my wife in labor to check in with them and that I went over every menu with them and answered all of their questions. I was also informed that the office was covering my position during the leave time that I earned having been employed with the company for over a year."

No answer was good enough for him. I excused myself out of his office and threw up outside. I felt weakened as though I had taken a gargantuan step backward with my health. The workplace became more and more toxic with these managers at the helm. I was working eighty-hour work weeks and commuting forty-five minutes each day to and from work. I was rewarded for this by being told to take inventory of the entire dining facility by myself.

The team atmosphere was virtually non-existent in this environment. I finished inventory passing out in the dry storage area. I was later awakened by a hard crash on the loading docks. Suddenly, I felt light headed. I ran to the restroom and threw up for almost an hour. This job which I had so much pride in at one point finally affected my health in the worst way possible. I felt as though the cancer was rearing its evil head and returned. Years of effort to rehabilitate my health and finally get on track with a career had come to a screeching halt. I thought, *if I can pull myself off of this floor, I will walk to the office and give my immediate notice. How can I take care of my sick wife and my baby if my health continues to dwindle here?*

What my boss did was illegal, I later discovered, but for now it was time to leave for good. The management in this kitchen was riding a sinking ship, and I was grabbing a life vest. I went over his head to his boss.

"Sir, I have to leave. My manager is not aware that I was on leave for my child's birth on the 17th of last month. He reprimanded me in spite of being informed that you all had been made aware in writing that I was leaving for FMLA. I am surrendering my badge and my pager. In short, I can no longer serve in this position and remain healthy for my family in this environment."

"Management is not as easy as you thought, right?" was his response.

I thanked all of my cooks and told them to keep up all of their hard work, cleaned out the office in which I had barely spent any time, and left corporate life forever. It had all happened so quickly, but we were free of this sulfuric atmosphere.

I went home that day to take care of Aileen, just as she had taken care of me. With a simple smile from my newborn son and a look from my wife, I wondered how I would break the news to my young family.

"I am through with excuses as to why I walk out that door every day with the hopes that I can make it better. I am determined to be by your side and make this better, whatever it takes. I will never walk out that door again to make that lonely forty-five minute trip to that hell hole again. I quit today. I do not want you to think this is not for the best. I lost my stomach today and everything in it because my manager asked me where I was when I took leave for Emerson's birth."

"You followed the protocol for family leave." Aileen responded.

"It doesn't matter," I told her, "we are going to get well together—me with my stomach and you with yours. I don't care how long it takes! And once we are better, we will pursue whatever life brings us."

"I love you Chuck," she said.

"I was born to run my own place and I will start a future for us just as soon as we get better together. We will make whatever sacrifices we need to, but I will never work in an environment like that again. We have come too far in our journey with my health for it to collapse over a career with a company like that!"

· CHAPTER 9 ·

NOW, IT'S MY TURN

It was time for me to cash in on any and all savings I had and slowly begin developing a business plan of my own. I spent countless hours on the internet and in the local Chamber of Commerce offices guiding a path for me along with my knowledge from other geographic regions. The region known as "The Triangle" has seen many layoffs over the last couple of years. I remember thinking that if Aileen and I played our cards right, we could ride this wave back up. Everyone has to eat, and so it was with great pride that we developed a local North Carolina small business called Hey, You're Worth It Catering. Aileen came up with the name on the way to get pizza one night. It was a great play on our last name. We catered using as much locally-sourced, organic, natural, and local food as possible. I spent my time developing our working relationships with farmers and suppliers and she would help while still healing at home. It was a time to develop our menus and signature dishes, all while reincorporating more solid foods like lean meats and fishes back into my diet. We offered samplings around the area at wellness events as well as in our home. Many of these brought us new clients, but mostly just enough to pay the bills.

One day the phone rang and it was my brother Mike. He was working on a television pilot and filming around North Carolina. He informed me that he had some great catering ideas for his shoot, and was wondering if we could "prepare a proposal." This was far more than just a catered lunch. It would involve providing all of the food for his production which included breakfast, lunch, snacks, and dinner. Known as "Craft Services," this would become an important facet of our business model. I arranged a barbecue for the cast and crew the night before shooting, an omelet bar for breakfast with juices, and a huge sandwich spread for lunch. We would purchase snacks from warehouse clubs. It would be a great hit. Aileen would coordinate from our home office, and I would pick up all necessary supplies and feed the cast and crew. This only lasted three days, but provided us with an insight into an industry which would help put us on the map. Aileen organized everything from the house and I was in the field cooking and serving the food. We would begin purchasing many items for our catering business across the state while renting many as well. I discovered the way to be successful as a part-time caterer was to know my limits. I did not begin looking into becoming a full-time caterer until I had been cancer-free for five years.

After that shoot, our phone began ringing with

film catering leads. By the time I had reached my five-year mark, Aileen and I were turning some business away. During this time, we worked a pilot, several major corporate commercials, and a major motion picture. We never strayed from our commitment to natural, local, and organic foods. Our clients knew this and we went from being just a licensed caterer/chef service to a preferred craft service/caterer with the North Carolina Film Commission.

We never stopped thinking of opening a physical location, but it became more and more obvious that building from the ground up would cost too much money, take too much time and cause too much aggravation. And so I went back to the drawing board and began seeking out turn-key restaurant spaces. It would take nearly two years, and then fate stepped in.

We found a space just a few blocks away from our home. It was abandoned but it had a lot of potential. Aileen would design and decorate and I would develop the menu. Seasonal catering menus consisted of ingredients from North Carolina and the southeastern region of the United States. We shortened "Hey, You're Worth It" to "Worth It Café" and opened on a bright March day. We would start out using the produce, meats, and cheeses from only about twelve local farms. With time, I used over a hundred different small businesses and farms from around the state. Unlike the various kitchens I worked in over the years before and after cancer, Aileen and I would nourish and mentor our staff members. We swore never to become like the managers at my university job I had quit years before. Every manager strives to create a family-like atmosphere in their kitchen. In the case of my chef, Jaime, I took a cook with very little knowledge of cooking from scratch and gave him a crash course in all things culinary. Over time, he learned kitchen safety, sanitation, equipment uses and more. We hired several other cooks, however the communication between my chef and I was paramount. We created inventory sheets, temperature sheets, grease trap checklists, and more to ensure a smooth and spit-polish-shined kitchen. Empowering employees became a very important part of our business model.

The unity of our kitchen kept our customers coming even during the difficult economic times. I recall having to re-examine the budget of the café several times a year after major catering clients laid off a percentage of their employees. With every downturn economically, we gradually saw increased business, not reduced. It was a sign that we had something very special. Fuel prices increased, followed by the bursting of the housing bubble, the financial crisis, and more. All the while, I found myself praying that a line would form at lunch and that we had customers calling for catering. I made sure to follow up on catering clients via email as much as I could. I believe many of our catering clients were very pleased to see that I delivered the catering as opposed to an employee. Attention to detail was a crucial point to navigating through the increasingly difficult market.

We had just made it through our second year of business when I was due for my 10-year cancer check-up. I was so nervous because of all I had been able to build in the past 10 years. We now had three children, a mortgage, and this business built with the passion of learning to taste solid foods again. This made the appointment particularly nerve-wracking. I remember arriving to the check-up with the spirit and mindset that we would persevere no matter what. Countless vials of blood were drawn, test and scans run, and I had a colonoscopy and endoscopy. Finally, the news—I was 10 years cancer-free, a particularly large hump to have arrived at. I dropped to my knees in joy and cried as I had never before. It was a time of great joy and reflection.

After word spread about the 10-year cancer-free date, I received quite a bit of publicity, but both Aileen's and my favorite attention to this day came from the visits we would receive from the families of cancer patients, or the patients themselves, at the restaurant nearly every day. No matter how busy my day was, I had no problem being the face of a survivor for people who were so in need of hope. I realized that Aileen and our family were not alone. We were a part of a cancer community, all of whom are living proof of a unified front to eliminate this disease. It remains to this day a humbling feeling.

Aileen, my great gift from above, has blessed me with three beautiful children, a house to call our home, and a business that we operated together for nearly seven years prior to selling it. My new career path led me to a nationally-produced television show, Thankfully Local with Chef Chuck, and now to my writing of this story. This one extraordinary person would help guide me through some difficult paths. Through every bump in the road towards recovery, she has been by my side.

· PART TWO ·

44 OF MY CANCER-FIGHTING RECIPES

To those struggling with this disease of cancer, I say surround yourself with love: the love of family, friends and other supporters. The more you have, the more likely you are to feel you have a reason to live. Cancer is no easy mountain to climb! Once you have reached the summit— remission or the removal of all cancer from your body— becoming a survivor and how you use your second chance at life is your gift to the world. My wish is that all cancer patients have enough strength to combat this horrible disease with all their might.

With my second chance, I am trying to give back by writing this resource guide as well as being a voice on television and the web for all cancer survivors. We can all make a difference in the cancer community. Don't feel sorry for yourself. Use your energy to help others struggling with this disease as a friend or just as a shoulder to lean on. Make a difference in your fellow cancer patients' lives.

They may in turn use their energy to do the same. Before you know it, we have made a huge impact in combatting this disease. Who knows? Our future efforts may even eradicate this disease from existence!

This book is equipped with an arsenal of resources in the form of recipes that have aided in my recovery. Be sure to consult your doctor and nutritionist about natural ways of healing yourself through the use of food and nutrition while undergoing treatments. Stay the course and know that many have come before you and you *can* beat this with the power of modern medicine and the energy supplied to you from the support of your friends and loved ones. Never, ever give up!

I am so grateful for life, so now please use me as an instrument to make a difference in all which is being done to annihilate this disease.

· THE LIQUID DIET ·

Looking back on my recovery, the last decade has had its ups and downs. During the nearly eight months of post-operation liquid diet, I tried to live like a normal guy in his twenties. I specifically remember asking a guy in the pizzeria if he could blend a pepperoni slice in a blender for me! This was a period of hell on Earth for me. The doctors and surgeons had pulled my entire digestive system apart and it was up to me to put it back together again. If I live to be one million, I would never want to see another medical shake again!

After I learned the hard way that liquid food with a straw was my only hope of seeing solid food again, I realized that broth, soft bananas and Florida avocados were not such a bad thing after all. I began experimenting with various types of protein and reminding my mother as well as myself that nearly every type of protein in the grocery store could be made into a stock: fish, turkey, chicken, and many others. It was in the early post-tumor days that my poor mother made two meals: one for a hungry household and one liquid form for me. The most basic meal for me started out with a large helping of the first recipe in this book—the veggie stock—and a large medical shake to which I would add banana slices to make it taste better! I can still taste that flavor today. For a guy who was given the odds I was, that was like a five-star meal. I later discovered the healing powers of yogurt/kefir and the power of coconut water. I was bound and determined to finish this liquid diet stage of my life on top in one of America's most beautiful cities—Miami!

Veggie Stock

INGREDIENTS

2 carrots, chopped

4-5 stalks of celery, chopped

1 large onion, chopped

1 leek, chopped, soaked in water (water discarded)

1 bell pepper, chopped

2-3 peppercorns, toasted

1 clove garlic

1 bunch thyme

1 bunch oregano

4 cups or more water

1 tsp grape seed oil

½ cup kosher salt (if salt sensitive, leave this out)

DIRECTIONS

1. Pre-heat a large sauce pot with oil and add veggies to pot.

2. Cook veggies until slightly softened.

3. Add water and bring to a boil.

4. Add all seasonings.

5. Simmer for at least an hour or up to 8 hours on low setting on stove.

6. Filter stock once desired color is achieved through a colander or china cap.

7. Can freeze for up to a year in freezer proof containers. (Allow to chill overnight in refrigerator prior to freezing.)

What can I say? I lived off of this stock for years after my recovery. I still find myself making this stock and even sharing it with friends who are struggling with this disease. Simply use whatever veggies you have laying around your refrigerator.

I refer back to this recipe whenever I'm not feeling well. It's extremely comforting to me, even now! The recipe is simple; just add your favorite cut of chicken to the veggie stock and you have my chicken stock. I used a lot of thigh and leg cuts for this stock which are inexpensive cuts with lots of flavor. Make sure to allow at least an hour and a half for the chicken to fully have cook and have its entire flavor absorbed into the stock. If you have the time, you should let it simmer for half a day or so. The chefs at school would grade us on the stocks appearance after a full 24 hours. I loved that class because the chef would let me take as much as I wanted home with me when he realized I'd rather not spend money on a can or box.

Chicken Stock

INGREDIENTS

1 pack of drumsticks
(about 5)
1 pack of thigh meat
(about 4)
2 carrots, chopped
4-5 stalks of celery, chopped
1 large onion, chopped
1 leek chopped, soaked in
water (water discarded)

1 bell pepper, chopped
2-3 peppercorns, toasted
1 clove garlic
1 bunch thyme
1 bunch oregano
4 cups or more water
1 tsp grape seed oil
½ cup kosher salt (if salt-
sensitive, leave this out)

DIRECTIONS

1. Pre-heat a large sauce pot with oil and add veggies to pot.

2. Cook veggies until slightly softened.

3. Add water and bring to a boil.

4. Add all seasonings.

5. Simmer for at least an hour or up to 8 hours on low setting on stove.

6. Filter stock once desired color is achieved through a colander or china cap.

The Mighty Miso Soup

INGREDIENTS

1 tbsp miso paste
2 green onions, chopped
$\frac{1}{8}$ block soft silken tofu, diced small

$\frac{1}{8}$ cup seaweed (You can rehydrate dried or omit. Miami had this fresh.)
3-4 cups hot water

DIRECTIONS

1. Heat water on stove top to a boil or in a tea kettle.

2. Combine all ingredients in a small bowl or on stove top once water is boiling.

3. Taste and add additional water if needed.

Not long after my return to Miami, a dear friend of mine introduced me to the beautiful world of Japanese sushi as well as the mighty miso soup that they serve in these sushi lounges in Miami. I know a lot of you would call me crazy for eating soup in a tropical climate like Miami, but put yourself in my shoes; one of your best friends tells you to come along and try it—and you do! She also would give regular reports to my parents who would pass them on to my physicians. Yes, my friends spied on me for my family (in a good way!) Although I was limited to the miso soup along with the occasional California roll, I am quite fond of the time I spent there. I spent many hours in North Carolina searching for great miso paste to make this soup in the earlier part of the decade. This is one I keep close. If you have a soy allergy or do not have access to a health food store or supermarket that carries miso, try this recipe with chicken or veggie stock.

Chilled Mango Soup

INGREDIENTS

4-5 large mangos

1 cup sour cream

1 cup white balsamic vinegar

2 tsp orange blossom honey

DIRECTIONS

1. Slice and pit mango.
2. In a blender, purée mango with honey for sweetness.
3. Add sour cream and continue puréeing.
4. Drizzle in vinegar delicately and slowly after sour cream is completely incorporated.
5. Serve in soup cups with slices of mango as a garnish.

I was not far past surgery when I met my wife. As part of a surprise to her family, she and I went to visit them in Puerto Rico. I immediately wanted to see all the beauty of the tropical island's farms. Yes, we wound up in the mercado *or farmer's market. It was here that I created my chilled mango soup in my mind. I still remember the looks that her family and neighbors gave when I made the soup the first time. Such seemingly unpairable ingredients, but then the brave soul to taste the first bite, wonderful!*

Orange Coco Agua Fresca

INGREDIENTS

Juice of 2 oranges
1 liter of coconut water
(1 large box or 2 large
coconuts)

¼ cup sugar (depends on
sweetness of coconut water)

DIRECTIONS

1. In a large pitcher, combine ingredients.
2. Refrigerate for up to one week.

---

*I have lived on coconut in its various forms for the better part of
a decade. Why buy other fluids? In Miami and most all Latin
or Asian markets, you will find fresh coconuts. I drank and still
drink my weight in coconut water. My fondest memory is of my
future father-in-law slicing them open with a machete off his
tree in Puerto Rico and more recently off his new tree in Florida.
I just love them! The water and flesh are the tastiest part. They
can be used as cups, decorations and many more. They have
tons of vitamins and electrolytes in them. Many studies are
being conducted around the world about their benefits. For me,
seasonal agua fresca made with coconut water, a fresh lime,
berry, orange, or mango juice has a multitude of benefits. The
beverage never gets old, and you can incorporate what is in
season into your drink. At first, everything tasted metallic to
me. I avoided this by adding a little fruit and some sugar agua
fresca. Traditionally this is like a tropical lemonade, but the
coconut water added much-needed nutrients and electrolytes.*

Key Lime Coco Agua Fresca

INGREDIENTS

Juice of 6-7 key limes or 3 Caribbean yellow limes

1 liter coconut water (1 large box or 2 large coconuts)

¼ cup sugar (depends on sweetness of coconut water)

DIRECTIONS

1. Combine ingredients in a large pitcher making sure to stir all of the juice and sugar together prior to adding the coconut water.

2. Serve over ice.

Can be used as a margarita mix when more sugar is added.

Summer Mango Agua Fresca

INGREDIENTS

½ cup mango purée
¼ cup sugar

1 liter coconut water
(in box or 2 fresh)

DIRECTIONS

1. Combine purée and sugar in a large pitcher until completely mixed.

2. Add coconut water to purée mix.

3. Serve over ice.

Strawberry Coco Agua Fresca

INGREDIENTS

½ cup strawberry purée
(about ½ pint of large,
fresh berries, ripe)

1 liter coconut water (1 large
box or 2 large coconuts)
¼ cup sugar (depends on
sweetness of coconut water)

DIRECTIONS

1. Combine ingredients in a large pitcher starting with the purée and the sugar. Add coconut after fully incorporated.

2. Serve over ice.

Needless to say: more sugar equals a fun strawberry daiquiri mix!

Strawberry Kefir

INGREDIENTS

1 cup kefir
½ pint strawberries, sliced
   and puréed
1 tbsp local honey or agave

1 tsp vanilla extract
¼ cup orange juice, freshly
   squeezed

DIRECTIONS

1. Combine ingredients in a blender and purée until completely mixed together.
2. Pour into cold glasses and garnish with fresh strawberry slices.

One thing about being on a liquid diet earlier in the decade and not juicing because of possible side effects is that I would eat and drink my weight in yogurt drinks. At first it was all that I could keep down, but later on, drinking a smoothie with friends helped me forget that it was a meal for me where it was a snack for the rest. Yogurt and in particular "kefir" with enzymes and various good bacteria for my new stomach was and still remains a very important part of my recovery. I have tried many of the flavors out their now, but for some reason adding my own fruit helps me control the flavor better. It is for this reason that I share these four recipes with plain kefir in mind. Most of your supermarkets carry kefir in the yogurt aisle. I use this probiotic to flush my digestive system on a regular basis. I recommend finding locally grown fruit where you live and freezing it for use in these drinks throughout the year.

Peach Kefir

INGREDIENTS

4 small peaches (about 1½ cup), sliced, pitted, and puréed

1 cup kefir

1 tsp lime juice

2 tbsp local honey

1 tsp vanilla extract

DIRECTIONS

1. Combine ingredients in a blender and purée until fully blended.

2. Pour into chilled glasses and garnish with fresh peach slices.

Citrus Cherry Kefir

INGREDIENTS

1 cup cherries, pitted and
  puréed

¼ cup organic sugar

¼ cup sweet red grapefruit
  juice

¼ cup orange juice

1 cup kefir

DIRECTIONS

1. Purée and blend ingredients in a blender until fully mixed.

2. Serve in a chilled, sugared glass with a slice of red
   grapefruit.

Apple Cinnamon Kefir

INGREDIENTS

1 cup fresh apple cider

½ cup kefir

1 tsp cinnamon (use your desired amount)

¼ cup fresh apple sauce

1 tsp (can use more depending on sweetness of sauce and
cider) local honey

DIRECTIONS

1. In a blender, blend ingredients until fully mixed.

2. Taste for desired sweetness. If needed add more honey.

3. Serve in a chilled glass with apple slices dipped in
cinnamon sugar on the rims of glass.

Chrysanthemum Tea Granita

INGREDIENTS

4 cups brewed chrysanthemum tea
2 tbsp orange blossom honey/tupelo honey

DIRECTIONS

1. Fully dissolve honey in tea and transfer to a glass casserole dish.
2. Freeze for up to 24 hours.
3. Scrape edges top to bottom regularly as ice forms with a fork.
4. Scrape mixture out of the dish and into chilled ice cream bowls.
5. Garnish with a sprig of fresh orange mint.

Granitas are simple to make and remarkably refreshing. Chrysanthemum tea is one of the greatest flavors I was introduced to while in Miami and it has healed me like no other tea could. I love the idea of combining something therapeutic, like the tea, with such a satisfying dessert.

Red Navel & Green Tea Granita

2 cups red navel juice
2 cups brewed green tea
¼ cup orange blossom honey or agave

DIRECTIONS

1. Blend and mix ingredients together in a large bowl.
2. Transfer to glass casserole dish and freeze for at least 8 hours in freezer.
3. Scrape into desired chilled bowls or cups and serve.

Low-Country
Cucumber Melon Granita

INGREDIENTS

1 personal watermelon
1 tsp local honey
2 English cucumbers, chopped

DIRECTIONS

1. Blend all in blender and transfer to chilled glass casserole dish.

2. Freeze for up to 8 hours depending on freezer.

3. Scrape desired amounts into chilled glasses and garnish with slices of cucumbers.

This was the very first thing I tried in what would become my "thankfully local" lifestyle. I would learn about seedless cucumbers grown in greenhouses in South Carolina coupled with refreshing local melons. June through August for nearly three years, this became a staple in my apartment.

Muscadine Granita

INGREDIENTS

4 cups muscadine grape juice

DIRECTIONS

1. Freeze juice in a casserole dish.
2. Scrape desired amounts into chilled cups or bowls.

Muscadine juice has many mystical powers of healing in the South. I never really had a taste for it growing up, although North and South Carolina have long been growing this native varietal for hundreds of years. High in antioxidants as well as vitamin C, I acquired a taste for this grape juice to enjoy the refreshment in the summer months during the course of my cancer recovery while living in the Charleston region of South Carolina. They needed no sweetening at all. The sugars from the grapes were and are plenty for me. Muscadine juice can be found in specialty stores around the South as well as natural food stores.

Classic Hummus

INGREDIENTS

1 cup cooked garbanzo beans
½ cup sesame paste/tahini
¼ cup fresh lemon juice
1 bunch oregano, stems discarded
Salt and pepper to taste

DIRECTIONS

1. Blend all ingredients in food processor until completely mixed.

2. Transfer mix to chilled bowl.

3. Store in refrigerator for up to three weeks.

Hummus and any version of great Mediterranean dips became huge during the late 1990s and early parts of the 2000s. This was the time when olive oils were springing up in every store and the Mediterranean diets as well as variations on low carbs were huge. What a time to be a vegan. These very easy dips became simple meals for my frail digestive system as I began the long and arduous journey of reintroducing solid foods back into my diet. Tahini paste (that amazing sesame seed paste traditionally used in hummus) can be subbed out for any number of nut butters such as peanut or almond, or even sunflower butter. Of course, when you eat hummus as much as I used to, one finds interesting ways to make hummus from what is on sale or cheaper than the classic ingredients.

During the course of my recovery I would revert back to liquid diets constantly. That being said, I have always considered dips and hummus to be liquids. Purée of... (continued on next page)

Southwestern Hummus

INGREDIENTS

8 ounces or 1 can cooked black beans
1 can chipotle sauce in adobo (or 1 fresh jalapeño)
¼ cup lime juice
Salt and pepper to taste

DIRECTIONS

1. Mix ingredients together in food processor.

2. Pulse to your preference in thickness.

3. Serve in a chilled bowl alongside cucumber wedges, organic veggies, or even pita.

(cont. from 114) ...fresh beans and oils with spikes of lemon juice or other citrus or acids such as vinegars are well known now in all Mediterranean restaurants and have proved to not only be light and filling, but flavorful too! Each hummus here has its own flavor characteristics. Making peanut butter as a base is a cool technique. Black beans and chipotles bring new life to the palate when you have to eat the same things over and over as I did. Try these recipes and more with your favorite foods. The idea is to incorporate lean, flavorful fats, as well as familiar flavors back into your diet. I did this when I was in the liquid diet stage because I do not consider them solid foods. Sometimes I like to serve hummus with veggies and baked pita wedges, as well as gluten-free rice crackers or cakes. Most nutritionists will advise to incorporate solids back into your diet slowly. As every case of cancer is different, please ask your nutritionist and doctor what types of foods (if any) are best for you.

Peanut Butter & Jelly Hummus

INGREDIENTS

1 can washed cooked Northern beans or white beans

2 cup unsalted peanuts

¼ cup peanut oil (I use Asian peanut oil because of the strong unrefined peanut taste)

2 tbsp agave

¼ cup strawberry jam

DIRECTIONS

1. In a food processor, pulse peanuts with peanut oil.

2. Once a paste is achieved, add agave and cooked beans and continue pulsing.

3. If mixture is too thick for your liking, add up to ¼ cup of chilled water until thinned out to your liking.

4. Transfer hummus to a chilled bowl and dollop strawberry jam into the center.

I was still a cancer patient when Aileen uttered the words to me, "We're pregnant!" I suppose I had to get better at this point. This recipe is dedicated to Emerson who loves his peanut butter and jelly. This is a creative way to eat it without bread.

Roasted Red Pepper Hummus

INGREDIENTS

1 jar roasted red peppers or 4 fresh, roasted and seeded
8 ounce local white beans (such as October/cranberry beans)
4 tbsp roasted garlic (about 4 cloves)
¼ cup tahini paste
1 bunch oregano stems, separated
Juice of 1 lemon plus zest
Salt and pepper to taste

DIRECTIONS

1. Pulse all ingredients in food processor to liking

2. Place in a chilled bowl and chill for at least an hour.

3. Serve with desired organic veggies and fruits or pita, or even gluten free crackers.

Smoked Eggplant Dip with Greek Yogurt & Herbs

INGREDIENTS

2 smoked eggplants
1 cup strained greek yogurt
1 bunch dill stems removed
Salt and pepper to taste

DIRECTIONS

1. Pulse all ingredients in a food processor.

2. Transfer to a chilled bowl and refrigerate for at least an hour.

3. Garnish with any remaining dill.

When eggplant was in season, I would often seek out the eggplant varietals that were the most meat-like and cook with them. One variety that I love is the "Black Beauty." I loved popping them in the smoker or on the grill with some wood chips for extra smoky flavor. At the time, there was no way I was able to eat any solid foods or meats that were smoked. With a little imagination and a meaty veggie like eggplant, I was able to eat these dips.

Mediterranean Roasted Eggplant Dip

INGREDIENTS

2 roasted eggplants
1 tbsp capers
2 roasted red peppers
¼ cup Kalamata olives
¼ cup olive oil
1-2 tbsp red wine vinegar

DIRECTIONS

1. In the food processor, pulse all ingredients together, slowly drizzling in olive oil and vinegar.
2. Serve chilled in bowl.

I would eat this pulsed veggies mix as a meal. Although I would pulse the veggies to a liquid state, I recommend you leave this dip as chunky as you like.

ADD ME SOME
VEGGIES, PASTAS, & WHOLE GRAINS
BACK

If it could be considered a victory, I remember when the doctor uttered these words: "Mr. Hayworth, it's okay for you to have some solid food again." Um, okay. What exactly did solid food mean? I discovered that night that there was a huge difference between what a guy in his twenties considered solid food and what a physician considered solid food! Thus the lesson of the next chapter—taking the term solid food slowly, especially when your digestive system has to completely rebuild itself. My body had to learn, along with my mind, what I could and could not eat. No meat proteins or fish proteins as of this point at all! So I learned the hard way that my diet would consist of mild and bland foods for the next few months. I would incorporate simple veggies, pastas and carbohydrates such as brown rice, and whole grains such as quinoa and bulgur wheat, and other soft starches and legumes. This was not easy for me. Anyone who is a regular meat eater: I challenge you to try it for a day, let alone the years I had to do it.

So, as I have informed many of my friends and customers over the years, I was a vegan! Although I consider these times in my recovery to be very difficult, I still find myself preparing these dishes several times a month as a reminder of how far I have come as well as a reminder of those who have struggled with GIST cancers and never made it as far as I have. In addition, I also recommend that even if you are a cancer patient whose body can digest meat proteins easily with your treatments, please try a vegetarian or vegan lifestyle as part of a holistic treatment for your body while undergoing heavy regiments of various treatments. Please discuss this with your doctors as well as nutritionists prior to making your final decision. This is a course that worked for me and my case.

Steamed Brown Rice with Quinoa & Peas

INGREDIENTS

1 cup brown rice dry
¼ cup quinoa
1 cup organic frozen peas
3 cups chicken stock

DIRECTIONS

1. Combine all ingredients except peas in a medium sauce pot and bring to a boil.

2. Once rice and quinoa are nearly fully cooked (about 45-50 minutes), add peas and fold into rice and quinoa mixture.

3. Serve hot or freeze for up to one year in freezer-proof bags.

Once I wised-up and realized that baby steps are the best options for me, the first solid food I ever ate and kept down was steamed brown rice and quinoa with peas. I would cook the brown rice and quinoa in chicken stock and add peas for protein because the peas would cook quickly in the rice and quinoa.

Root Veggie Boil

INGREDIENTS

1 large turnip, peeled and diced
4-6 peeled red potatoes or Yukon Gold
3-4 cups vegetable stock
1 tbsp veggie margarine/vegan butter substitute
1 bunch flat leaf parsley (preferably organic)

DIRECTIONS

1. Bring stock and veggies to a boil until softened.

2. Strain and add margarine and parsley.

3. Serve with your favorite meal steaming hot!

Simple boiled potatoes and turnips nearly saved my life! After being so adventurous and falling hard time and time again with my digestion being way beyond out of whack, sometimes I would eat a piece of humble pie and prepare this simple dish for myself and feasted for at least two meals on it. I know, it seems so bland! Again journey back with me to a time where the internet really did not have all the answers and social media was virtually non-existent. I had to rely on my own scientific hypothesizes as to whether or not something would work for me to eat or not. By the way, at first it was very bland, but at least it was food! I used my Nana's parsley to help aid in my recovery. Also, I discovered great veggie margarine as well!

Florida Avocado & Citrus Salad

INGREDIENTS

1 Florida avocado, sliced and pitted
2 red navels, segmented
1 red onion, sliced and julienned

DIRECTIONS

1. Arrange all ingredients on a platter

2. Serve to waiting guests

3. Avocado may need some fresh lemon juice if not serving right away.

This next dish was a challenge to me. Here Chuck, try an avocado and an orange from my tree. What was I going to say? I absolutely love the sweetness of a Florida or tropical avocado. You may be able to find them in your local super market. The combination of my first orange post-liquid diet with the creamy, sweet avocado and, for kicks, some amazing sweet red onion make this salad a memorable dish for me.

Zucchini & Carrot Noodle Salad

INGREDIENTS

½ cup sesame ginger sauce

2 carrots, sliced on mandoline or thinly julienned

2 zucchinis, sliced on mandoline or julienned

1 tbsp fresh ginger for garnish

1 bunch cilantro, chopped (for garnish)

DIRECTIONS

1. Combine all ingredients except ginger and cilantro in a bowl.

2. Toss until veggies are fully coated with sauce.

3. Garnish with julienned ginger and chopped cilantro.

4. This dish can marinate for up to a few days in the refrigerator. When veggies are in season, only make what you need as they will get soggy quickly.

Admittedly, it was during this time in my life that I experimented with the "raw" diet. I would make veggie noodles out of about every veggie I could get my hands on at school. This next recipe was my absolute favorite. Tender, fresh zucchini marries with fresh, sweet, crisp carrot and a sesame ginger sauce for an explosion of flavor in your mouth! I love this one for those nauseous nights where I just needed something light to eat for dinner. I found that the raw diet of this time period in my life actually helped me regain my sense of taste that was burned away by a constant metallic taste in my mouth which was, and is, a common side effect of most medications prescribed to me.

Roasted Red Pepper Pasta

INGREDIENTS

2 ½ cups roasted red peppers, chopped

2-3 large eggs

3 cups unbleached AP flour

3-4 tsp fresh roasted garlic

3-4 tsp onion powder

1-2 tsp fresh ground pepper

2 tsp kosher salt

3 tsp cornmeal

DIRECTIONS

1. Combine all ingredients in a bowl and knead dough by hand or use the food processor technique.

2. Cut into pieces and roll out onto floured surface with some flour and corn meal.

3. Cut into desired shapes or sizes and cook as desired.

I found that reading food labels became somewhat of an art. I love when dry pasta has a hundred ingredients in it! Pasta should have flour, eggs, and maybe veggie purée—that's it! Keep an eye out for ingredients in your food. Preservatives are the enemy for me. I decided after much experimentation to make fresh pasta. What type could I keep down? I started with a basic egg and flour with a little corn meal. After that, purées of spinach, tomatoes, herbs, and peppers. This recipe is one of my favorites, roasted red pepper pasta. I like adding a little heat with some fresh ground pepper towards the end that added a little heat to this. If you are sensitive, you can feel free to leave it out. This dough can also freeze in freezer-proof bags for up to a year if you do not use it all right away. It is a great way to use peppers while they are in season and inexpensive in your local farmers market.

Tofu Chili Noodle Bowl with Shaved Ginger & Veggies

INGREDIENTS

1 package fresh whole wheat noodles or soba noodles (commonly found in Asian markets)

1 package firm tofu block

2 cups or more miso broth

2 green onions, chopped

2 carrots, julienned on mandoline or diced small

1 tbsp Asian chili paste (such as sriracha)

1½ cup fresh spinach (curly leaf if available)

2-3 strips of ginger, shaved on mandoline

DIRECTIONS

1. In a large sauce pot, bring miso to a heavy simmer and add veggies.

2. As veggies cook, dice tofu into chunks.

3. Add ginger to soften and add flavor.

4. Add tofu and noodles and cook in miso broth until noodles are fully cooked.

5. Serve in hot bowls.

Say what you want about the soy industry around the world, soy was and is still a staple in my diet! I do not mean that bottle at the restaurant on the side of the table. I am talking about tofu, edamame, veggie protein (TVP), soy flour, soy milks and creams, and the list goes on and on. If I do not eat one form of soy a week post-cancer, I am not living! Early on in my recovery, noodle bowls became a staple in my diet after I was sure I could digest the basics of solid foods. I also explored the healing powers of chili during my recovery.

Tofu Cacciatore

INGREDIENTS

1 pint cremini mushrooms
1 sweet onion, sliced and diced
2 tbsp garlic
1 bunch oregano, chopped
1 bell pepper, chopped into strips
1 can organic tomatoes, chopped
2 tbsp olive oil
1 package firm tofu

DIRECTIONS

1. Pre-heat a large non-stick skillet with olive oil.
2. Add garlic and veggies along with the tomatoes.
3. While pan comes to a full simmer, chop tofu slices into thick slices.
4. Once pan has begun to simmer, add tofu.
5. Serve, once tofu is fully heated through, in bowls.

So this one evening, I was craving one of my favorite dishes—chicken cacciatore—and my loving fiancée (now wife), Aileen, told me, "no way!" Keep in mind at this point I had not had any significant portion of meat in several years. I was taking prescription-strength iron pills and had no strength. Needless to say, we compromised with this next dish: tofu cacciatore. All the great veggies including peppers, onions, mushrooms, tomatoes, only without the chicken.

Vegan tomato pie came out of my craving for that Southern classic, tomato pie. I had no way to digest such a heavy dish. That was until I learned of the use of soy aioli and rice-based cereals and soy cheddar. Natural food stores were everywhere in South Florida as well as Charleston. You just needed to know where they were! This recipe incorporated my favorite rice cereal, Chex, with juicy ripe tomatoes and the creamy vegan aioli. Couple that with a cheese that tasted as close to the real thing as I was going to get. It was a great recipe to have as a meal for a while. Slice individual pieces and freeze for a quick bite for lunch.

Vegan Tomato Pie

INGREDIENTS

½ cup vegan lite mayo

¼ cup soy cheddar cheese

1 ripe heirloom tomato, sliced

2 cups Rice Chex cereal

2 cups Corn Chex cereal

½ cup coconut oil solids

Sea salt and pepper to taste

DIRECTIONS

1. In a food processor, combine cereals and coconut oil solids and season with salt and pepper to liking.

2. Transfer mix to an oiled pie dish/tin.

3. Puncture mixture several times with a paring knife to keep from rising too much.

4. Pre-heat oven to 375°.

5. Bake pie dish for 8-10 minutes depending on oven until slightly browned.

6. Remove and let cool.

7. In a mixing bowl, combine mayo and cheese.

8. Scoop the mixture into a pie dish/tin and spread across using a spoon or rubber spatula.

9. Top mixture with tomato slices and additional cheddar if needed.

I like using fresh chopped herbs as well with this. Another idea is to add what you have left of the soy cheddar in the bag, once using the amount called for in the recipe, to the dough. It makes for a nice "cheesy" bite.

Along with soy, legumes were a vital source of protein throughout my recovery. These recipes were a way to start eating legumes again, southwestern style. Chili peppers and chili sauces (without preservatives) were integral in my recovery. Here are a few recipes that I found truly helpful when I was invited to BBQs and parties. I would just bring them along (with enough to share, of course) so that I could enjoy the event without getting sick from eating something too heavy or harsh on my digestive system.

Fried Pink-Eyed Peas

INGREDIENTS

3 tsp cayenne seasoning
1 tsp paprika
4-6 tbsp peanut oil
1 pound fresh (or frozen) pink-eyed peas
Sea salt and pepper to taste
Zest and juice of 1 naval orange

DIRECTIONS

1. In a small bowl, combine cayenne, paprika, and desired salt and pepper. Set aside.

2. Pre-heat a skillet large enough for beans, add peas and crisp until golden brown.

3. Transfer to a plate lined with paper towels to drain briefly.

4. Place into bowl once drained.

5. Toss in seasonings and zests and serve warm.

This makes a great snack while watching a movie or sports on TV.

Legume & Jicama Salad

INGREDIENTS

1 jicama, peeled and sliced thin
2 spring onions, sliced and chopped
8 ounces cooked black beans
1 red bell pepper, chopped
1 sweet potato, sliced thin
Zest and juice of 2 limes
Zest and juice of 1 navel orange
1 tbsp agave or orange blossom honey
Salt and pepper to taste

DIRECTIONS

1. Toss all ingredients in a chilled large mixing bowl.

2. Serve chilled.

Jicama and citrus marry beautifully in this salad, especially sweet potato. If you have never eaten sweet potato raw, give it a try. It has more sweetness than carrots, and they are locally grown where I live! This salad is a perfect mix of home and the exotic ingredients from South Florida (my home away from home while at school).

Veggie Burgers

INGREDIENTS

2 cups cooked beluga lentils
1 cup cooked quinoa or bulgur wheat
2 spring onions, chopped
1 bell pepper, chopped
2 tbsp toasted cumin ground
1 tsp cayenne pepper
1 tsp lime juice
Salt and pepper to taste
1 tbsp olive oil

DIRECTIONS

1. In a bowl combine cooked beluga lentils with quinoa, chopped onion, and pepper.

2. Mix ingredients until onions and peppers are evenly spread throughout mixture.

3. Form into patties.

4. Pre-heat skillet with olive oil.

5. Sear veggie burgers until golden brown on each side.

Spinach Paneer

INGREDIENTS

1 box frozen organic spinach
1 teaspoon Canola oil
1 can coconut milk
6 tbsp madras curry

½ block of queso blanco or
   local farmers cheese round
Garlic and onion powder to
   taste
Salt and pepper to taste

DIRECTIONS

1. Bring a large sauce pot on medium setting with oil and add spinach and cook until fully heated through.

2. Add coconut milk and season with curry seasoning.

3. Stir until appears to be creamed spinach.

4. Add cheese and seasonings to taste.

5. Serve over basmati rice.

These are some simple ways to make tomato and spinach paneers. These are known as saag and makhani paneers. A homestyle version of these only requires what you have in your pantry and local super markets or farmer's markets: good organic veggies and fruits and local cheeses. These are easy to find. I used queso blanco from a Latin market to make mine, but if you can find a local farmer's cheese made by a local farm, try that. It really brings all the flavors together nicely. Dairy was something I had only in the form of yogurt. When Aileen suggested Indian food, I must admit that I was nervous. Paneer has always remained a staple in my diet since she introduced me to Indian food and its many amazing veggie and lean meat protein uses.

Tomato Paneer

INGREDIENTS

1 can crushed organic tomatoes

1 can coconut milk

6 tbsp madras curry

½ block of queso blanco or local farmers cheese round

Garlic and onion powder to taste

Salt and pepper to taste

DIRECTIONS

1. In a blender, combine tomatoes, coconut milk, and curry.

2. Transfer to a large pot and bring to a simmer.

3. Add queso blanco and or local farmer's cheese.

4. You may choose to add hot chili powder at this point. I omitted it. Add seasonings and taste.

5. I suggest grilling some simple veggies and serving over basmati rice.

A little different this time. I think you will appreciate the simplicity!

Desserts (as great as they are) did not sit well in my stomach. The fact is that I was eating so little when I was first recovering that little bite sized desserts were all that I could manage. It was good enough for many of my friends who were pastry chefs and students. My challenge to many since has been to let folks taste the light sweet finish to their meals. The classic French custards and torts and such just did not work for me. I found myself experimenting with all varieties of different light desserts and ingredients I had never used or eaten before such as silken tofu and Greek yogurt. Simple compotes and panna cottas were all it took to get a little something sweet without feeling overly full.

Lemon Tofu Panna Cotta

INGREDIENTS

1 box silken tofu (firm, 12.3 ounces)
4 tsp agar agar (found in natural food stores or Asian stores)
3 tsp arrowroot (found in natural food stores)
Zest of 1 lemon
1 tsp vanilla extract
1 tbsp agave or more

DIRECTIONS

1. Over a double boiler, combine tofu and agar agar.

2. Once they have been completely combined and incorporated at liquid state, thicken with arrowroot.

3. Add zests and extract.

4. Sweeten with agave to your liking.

5. Transfer to custard cups and chill for several hours at minimum before serving.

The longer this dessert has to set, the creamer and more similar to its gelatin counterpart.

Sweet Potato Panna Cotta

INGREDIENTS

2 cups sweet potato butter

2 cups greek yogurt

1 cup local honey

1 pouch unflavored gelatin

DIRECTIONS

1. In a medium sized sauce pan, combine ingredients

2. Bring mixture to a simmer being careful to not burn or curdle mix and making sure all ingredients are mixed all the way through.

3. Pour mixture into small custard cups and chill for about two hours or until solid.

4. Serve chilled and enjoy!

I first made this dish for a friend who wanted to use the restaurant for a dinner he was hosting for his office. I wanted to do something with the sweet potato butter I had made for a client earlier in the week. I knew this one would work because of the purple sweet potatoes I made the butter with. They add such a beautiful color to the plate. Truth be told it was the first of many times I would use gelatin in this recipe as opposed to agar agar. Try both the agar agar and the gelatin and let me know which you prefer.

Apple Compote with Streusel Topping

INGREDIENTS

2 cups chopped apples

1 cup sugar

1 tsp cinnamon

2 tbsp butter

2 teaspoons Canola oil

¼ cup brown sugar

½ cups unbleached AP flour

DIRECTIONS

1. Pre-heat oven to 350°.

2. Heat a medium-sized sauce pot with Canola oil.

3. Add apples, sugar, and cinnamon and adjust to medium-high heat.

4. Once apple solution is sautéing on stove top, combine brown sugar, flour and butter in a small mixing bowl.

5. This mixture should be about penny-sized to top the finished compote.

6. Once thickened, transfer apple mixture to individual pie tins or to a large, oiled casserole dish.

7. Top apple mix with flour mixture and bake for 10-12 minutes or until flour/streusel mix is golden brown.

8. Serve right away.

I recommend placing this dessert in your oven right as your family is finishing dinner. It can be made ahead and placed in the icebox for use later that evening.

I MADE IT!
INCORPORATING MEATS & FISH
BACK INTO MY DIET

I suppose having grown up a meat eater, I felt a little weird about being a vegan and vegetarian for half a decade or so. I found myself reminding my friends when we had the opportunity to dine out that I need a vegetarian option. My wife has constantly searched for options for all of us to eat vegetarian at least once a week. I remember the day I took the plunge and brought fish back into my diet. I knew that I was a long way from a porterhouse steak and a baked potato, but it felt great! I was living in Charleston, South Carolina right off of Meeting Street. Aileen wanted the freshest seafood from the docks. What was I going to tell her, no?

We later started weaning me onto meat with chicken and rice soups and simple grilled chicken breasts with lemon juice. It was during this time that I began eating only natural and organic meats with an emphasis on locally grown. I have learned to this day that the best meats for you are the leaner cuts of meat and protein, many of which I have included in this section. Hopefully I can give you some great ideas that you may not have tried before in your diet.

I have had many scares in the past several years, some legitimate some not, but I have always turned to the comfort on those days of chicken and rice soup. Many Americans would drop this soup in favor of chicken noodle, but I just love the way it feels in my stomach after a day of drinking chalk x-ray and IV fluid that leave a metallic taste in your mouth for days. Follow that up with a pint of blood being drawn from your body and tested for iron levels and God knows what else. Oh, the memories! I had never felt so alone until Aileen started coming with me to the half-day affairs. Somehow the fear would roll in knowing that I have someone who I was going to marry and loved me literally through sickness and health. She would be the first one to see me through all of these times, the thick and thin, and meet me on the heaven side of hell with a kiss, embrace and this soup at times. That was all it would take. That is still all it takes to get me through the toughest of days.

This will freeze well for up to a year, y'all! Use of leftover chicken and rice from last night's dinner is encouraged with this dish.

Chicken & Rice Soup

INGREDIENTS

2 poached chicken breasts, bone and skin removed (free range and organic)
2 cups white rice cooked
2 carrot peeled and chopped
1 sweet onion, chopped
4 celery stalks, chopped
6 cups chicken stock
1 tsp Canola oil

DIRECTIONS

1. Pre-heat a large sauce pot with Canola oil.
2. Add veggies and render until onion reaches caramelized stage.
3. Add chicken and rice at the same time.
4. Once chicken is reheated, add stock and bring to a boil.

You may wish to add seasoning (like salt, pepper or Italian herb seasoning). At this point in my recovery, most of my meat dishes were quite bland. It freezes great, y'all.

Oh, for the chef in me to taste the flavor of grilled meat again. Early on for me, chicken was all I could keep down. So every barbecue I visited and every steakhouse (and all the other functions you can think of involving a grill) wound up having my plate covered in grilled chicken. I apologize to all whom I annoyed with this gesture of sometimes bringing my own boneless, skinless chicken to your functions. I suppose now as time goes by you have forgiven me as I never revealed that I was battling stomach cancer at the time. I used chilies during this time that were locally grown to combat any germs going around, as my immune system was not quite back to normal and would not become so for many years to come.

Grilled Chicken with Black Bean Salsa

INGREDIENTS

4 boneless, skinless chicken breasts

1 tbsp olive oil

1 bunch oregano, chopped

2 tsp onion powder

2 tsp garlic powder

Salt and pepper to taste

¼ cup lemon juice

4 tbsp Worcestershire sauce

1 can black beans (or 1 pound, seasoned and cooked)

1 red onion, diced small

1 jalapeño ripe (diced small)

5-6 grape tomatoes, sliced in half

1 bunch cilantro, chopped

Juice of 2 limes

DIRECTIONS

1. In a blender, blend oil, seasonings, oregano, and Worcestershire sauce.

2. Place in a large bowl and coat chicken with marinade.

3. Preheat grill and spray.

4. Make sure that chicken is coated with all ingredients, grill until internal temperature reaches 165° (time depends on thickness of chicken breasts)

5. While chicken is grilling, combine beans, onion, jalapeño, tomatoes, and cilantro in a large bowl and toss to mix.

6. Juice the two limes and mix into salsa.

7. Once chicken has finished grilling, let rest for a few minutes on a platter wrapped in foil.

8. Top each chicken breast with a spoonful of salsa and serve.

I am often asked what types of fish I ate when I first started eating fish again. At first, simple, flaky fish such as flounder and tilapia were the easiest options for me. Aileen would laugh at me because I would plate her masterpieces and my plate would be so simple. She later realized that I was not eating nearly as much as most folks our age. It was only a few years later that I could return to eating heavier fish such as tuna or, as you will read next, pecan-crusted salmon.

Broiled Tilapia with Vegan Beurre Blanc Sauce

INGREDIENTS

4 organic tilapia fillets
1 zest lemon whole
3-4 tsp chopped dill
1 tsp chili flake
1 tbsp grape seed oil
Salt and pepper to taste

1 cup egg replacer,
   reconstituted using
   vegetable stock
¼ to ½ cup lemon juice or
   orange juice
1 tbsp whole grain mustard (or
   more depending on taste)

DIRECTIONS

1. Preheat grill or broiler to medium-high.

2. In a mixing bowl, season fish with dill, one half tablespoon of oil, chili flake, salt, pepper, and zest to taste.

3. Using oil spray, coat aluminum foil sheets that measured to the length and width of the fish fillets.

4. Fold foil around the fish creating a boat. Or, fold over and create a blanket-like fold for the fish.

5. Transfer to a sheet pan or oven-safe dish.

6. Broil/grill on cooler side of oven until it reaches 120°-130°, depending on desired level of doneness.

7. While fish is cooking, in a small sauce pot combine egg substitute, mustard, remaining zest, and juice and bring to a simmer, carefully stirring with a whisk.

8. Unwrap fish and carefully remove from foil. This can be done as part of presentation to guests while passing sauce for guests to scoop onto their plates.

Pecan-Crusted Salmon with Steamed Veggies

INGREDIENTS

4 pieces salmon filets, skin off

4 large eggs

2 cups unbleached AP flour

5 cups crushed pecans

Salt and pepper to taste

1 small cauliflower, sliced into pieces

½ red onion, sliced roughly

6-8 asparagus, sliced

1-2 carrots, peeled and sliced on a bias

DIRECTIONS

1. Preheat oven to 350°.

2. Place flour, eggs, and pecans in three separate mixing bowls.

3. Fluff egg using a fork or whisk such as you were preparing scrambled eggs.

4. Season each bowl with salt and pepper.

5. Coat salmon filets in seasoned flour, brushing off any excess.

6. Next roll each salmon filet in egg solution.

7. Transfer egg and flour-coated salmon to the bowl of pecans and roll each fillet in pecan mixture. It may be necessary to lightly press pecans onto surface of salmon.

8. Place pecan-crusted salmon onto a parchment-lined sheet pan and bake for about 10 minutes, each side. (Time may differ depending on thickness of filet and desired doneness.)

9. After 10 minutes, flip filets and bake for another 10 minutes.

10. Prepare steamer on stove top and steam veggies.

11. Remove salmon from oven and allow to rest.

12. Plate on top of steamed veggies.

Buffalo Sliders

INGREDIENTS

1 pound grass-fed local bison
or beef

1 package dinner rolls

1 tbsp ground cumin

1 tbsp onion powder

1 tbsp garlic powder

1/2 tsp smoked paprika

Lettuce, ketchup, tomatoes,
sliced red onion

DIRECTIONS

1. In a large mixing bowl, combine meat with seasoning.

2. For sliders, try to keep within about $^1/_8$ pound meat portions (they can come back for seconds).

3. Sear burgers to desired temperature on a pre-heated grill.

4. Toast buns alongside the meat.

5. Serve with desired sauces and toppings.

My GI doctors recommended lean proteins and whole grains and to research this first, as they were not nutritionists and every body heals differently. I decided to take a walk through my local farmer's markets and ask my friends, the farmers, for recommendations. They suggested a fairly new animal in the market—buffalo—which would become a great friend to me. Buffalo meat is packed with vitamins and minerals and one of the leanest meats becoming available in The Carolinas and the Southeast. At this point in my recovery, I could not go anywhere near beef, but found myself craving red meat. This was probably due to my low iron levels. If you have never tried it, I invite you to try it in this slider recipe where we replaced traditional ground beef with ground bison/buffalo. Yummy mini burgers make this recipe a great one for the whole family and it will be our secret that they are not beef!

Chuck's Lettuce Wraps

INGREDIENTS

1 pound lean, ground turkey

¼ cup grated ginger

¼ cup garlic, chopped

1-1½ cups water chestnuts, chopped

2 bunches green onions, chopped

Fried noodles/chow mein noodles/fried lo mein (for crunch and garnish)

3 tbsp Canola oil

⅛ cup teriyaki sauce

2 heads of Boston Bibb or other lettuces

DIRECTIONS

1. In a medium sized wok, combine ginger and garlic and cook until slightly browned.

2. Add ground turkey. After the turkey is cooked, add water chestnuts and green onions.

3. Make sure most of the moisture is gone from the pan and add the sauce.

4. Garnish mix with noodles and let guests pick lettuce and other toppings such as peanuts, cilantro, and shaved onion.

Using lean, ground turkey, I continued with the advice of my GI doctors and created this next dish. If you do not fancy turkey, you can try chicken or lean pork. I have found that I cannot eat this dish when dining out because of the amount of oil that most restaurants use to prepare it. Aileen loves this version as it feeds our crowd on game day and some nights just a group of hungry kids!

Lemon-Skewered Chicken & Veggies

INGREDIENTS

1 pound boneless chicken
breasts or boneless thigh
meat, skinless, sliced

¼ cup fresh or dried oregano,
chopped

½ cup olive oil

1 tbsp Worcestershire sauce

¼ cup lemon juice

1 tbsp onion powder

1 tbsp garlic powder

Sea salt and pepper to taste

DIRECTIONS

1. In a blender, pulse all ingredients except chicken and season with salt and pepper.

2. Pour in a glass casserole dish or plastic bag and add chicken.

3. Allow to marinate for a few hours, chilled in the icebox.

4. Soak wooden skewers in hot water for at least 1 hour.

5. Remove marinated chicken and skewer.

6. Cook on grill or pre-heated grill pan until internal temperature reaches 165° or higher using a meat thermometer. (Usually about 10 minutes each side, depending on thickness of chicken.)

You hear so many Mediterranean diet health tips. Aileen turned me on to leaner Greek foods while we were in Charleston. Lemon-skewered chicken and veggies is a great version of the wonderful clean and fresh flavors that Mediterranean foods have provided in my recovery.

Greek Lamb Kabobs

INGREDIENTS

1 pound lean ground lamb
¼ cup feta cheese
1 tbsp dried oregano
Salt and pepper to taste

1 English cucumber, rough
    diced
2 cloves roasted garlic
¼ cup strained Greek yogurt
1 bunch dill

DIRECTIONS

1. In a bowl, mix lamb with feta cheese and oregano with desired amounts of salt and pepper.

2. Pre-heat indoor grill pan.

3. Use soaked skewers and mold meat around the skewers in an oval motion.

4. Sear/grill until you reach your desired doneness.

5. While meat is grilling, purée strained Greek yogurt with garlic, cucumber, and dill.

6. Serve grilled lamb kabob with sauce or over sautéed greens or couscous.

Lamb is something that has grown on me in my recovery. I hated it prior to cancer but absolutely love it now! Simple, local, grass-fed Carolina lamb in a gyro or even a simple skewer as I have here makes for a great light dinner. You can pair it with a Greek yogurt cucumber sauce or just eat it plain over a sauté of organic greens and garlic. It makes for a yummy dinner either way. The key is to select lean ground lamb by talking with farmers who raised the lamb. The leaner, the better! This is especially true in recovery from stomach cancer.

Couscous with Orange Juice & Herbs

INGREDIENTS

1 cup whole wheat couscous
2 cups fresh squeezed orange juice
¼ cup veggie stock

DIRECTIONS

1. Bring juice to a boil with the stock and add couscous.

2. Turn stove off and let couscous absorb liquid.

3. Serve hot or chilled depending on preference.

This is a great side for the previous dish as it is light and flavorful. It also pairs well with Mediterranean foods.

Seared Tuna

INGREDIENTS

2 fresh tuna steaks
2 blood oranges, zested and segmented
1 bunch arugula
Sea salt and pepper to taste
1 tbsp rice wine vinegar
1 tbsp olive oil

DIRECTIONS

1. In a small bowl, combine salt and pepper with zest.

2. Season tuna with a little oil and some of seasoning.

3. Preheat a skillet with about a half teaspoon of oil.

4. Sear tuna in pan on each side.

5. In a separate bowl, toss arugula with oil, vinegar, and remaining salt and pepper mix.

6. Remove tuna and top with tossed arugula.

7. Garnish with segments of blood oranges.

Aileen would not let me complete this story of love, patience and recovery without including these next citrus recipes. Tuna of all varieties has become a staple on many low-country menus across Charleston. On occasion, when the tuna was running, I made her a great meal with simply fresh citrus and the tuna itself. I also used some fresh arugula and olive oil.

Sautéed Greens with Roasted Garlic

INGREDIENTS

1 pound spinach
1 bunch swiss chard, sliced
1 bulb roasted garlic
Salt and pepper to taste
1 tsp olive oil

DIRECTIONS

1. Pre-heat skillet with oil.

2. Add greens and wilt while slowly adding roasted garlic and desired amount of salt and pepper.

3. Remove once spinach and swiss chard have wilted to desired amount.

A variation of this involves cooking the segments with a little sugar and making them into quenelles of blood orange.

For Tanya, I dedicate this last sweet dessert. It is a version of the orange semifreddo we had at our lunch. The key to a great warm weather summer dessert is keeping it light. I use a local pecan crust with tangerine juice and custard pulled together and chilled with a little cream and plain gelatin. I like to chill it for a few hours at minimum or up to a day to make sure it is served chilled.

You can also garnish this refreshing dessert with fresh tangerine slices. I love the Florida tangelos when they are in season. A lighter version of this is to use same ratios of Greek yogurt and gelatin in a panna cotta style. I have also used egg substitute in place of whole eggs in the recipe and it works out great. Be sure to follow directions on the package if using egg substitute to dilute properly.

Orange Semifreddo

INGREDIENTS

½ cup semolina flour

4 ½ cups ground pecans

1 ½ stick melted butter or
  1 cup coconut oil solids
  (amount depends on brand)

½ cup organic sugar

4 eggs, whisked

2 cups heavy cream

1 cup tangerine juice

1 pouch unflavored gelatin
  OR 2 tsp agar agar

1 tangerine segmented or
  seedless orange

6-8 mint leaves (I use what I
  have in the garden.)

DIRECTIONS

1. Pre-heat oven to 375°

2. In a food processor, pulse pecans with semolina flour and melted butter/coconut oil.

3. Transfer dough mixture to a spring form pan and bake until solid golden brown about 20-25 minutes depending on oven.

4. Set this pan aside and allow to cool.

5. Over a double boiler with simmering water, combine eggs, cream, 1/4 cup of sugar, and juice.

6. Once desired thickness is achieved, sprinkle in gelatin/agar agar.

7. Stir in mixture until incorporated fully, and place in refrigerator for at least three hours or up to 24 hours until mixture is solid.

8. Remove from pan and slice into individual slices.

9. Garnish individual slices with mint leaves.

· THANK YOU ·

Thank you all for your support over the years, especially those who have not lived to see this come to fruition. I will see you all when the day breaks for me at the gates. Until then, stay strong for me and watch over us.

Visit Chuck online at

www.TheChefsRecovery.com

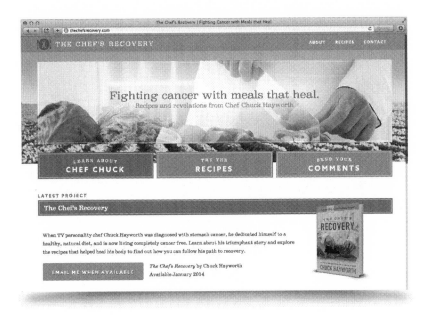

- Learn about Chuck's upcoming projects
- Explore and try many more recipes
- Purchase additional copies
- Share your thoughts on the book!